The Invisible World

Also by Anthony DeStefano

A Travel Guide to Heaven

Ten Prayers God Always Says Yes To:

Divine Answers to Life's Most Difficult Problems

The Invisible World

Understanding Angels, Demons, and

the Spiritual Realities That Surround Us

Anthony DeStefano

Doubleday

New York   London   Toronto   Sydney   Auckland

DD

DOUBLEDAY

Published in the United States by Doubleday Religion, an imprint of the
Crown Publishing Group, a division of Random House, Inc., New York.

www.crownpublishing.com

www.doubledayreligion.com

DOUBLEDAY and the DD colophon are registered trademarks of
Random House, Inc.

Cataloging-in-Publication Data is on file with the Library of Congress.

ISBN 978-0-385-52223-6

eISBN 978-0-307-72080-1

PRINTED IN THE UNITED STATES OF AMERICA

Design by Leonard Henderson

Cover design by Andy Schmalen / Schmalen Design, Inc.

1 3 5 7 9 10 8 6 4 2

First Edition

This book is dedicated to my grandmothers,

Elisa Pesiri DeStefano (1900–1956)

and

Vita Simone (1909–1984)

There are more things in heaven and earth, Horatio,

Than are dreamt of in your philosophy.

—Shakespeare, *Hamlet,* 1.5., 166–67

Contents

CHAPTER 1: THE HAUNT DETECTOR   13

CHAPTER 2: THE INVISIBLE GOD   24

CHAPTER 3: INVISIBLE HELPERS:

THE WORLD OF THE ANGELS   42

CHAPTER 4: INVISIBLE EVIL:

THE DEVIL AND HIS DEMONS   61

CHAPTER 5: THE INVISIBLE SOUL   82

CHAPTER 6: INVISIBLE WARFARE:

THE DIABOLICAL BATTLE FOR SOULS   100

CHAPTER 7: INVISIBLE GRACE   124

CHAPTER 8: THE INVISIBLE POWER OF SUFFERING   142

CHAPTER 9: INVISIBLE DESTINY:

DEATH, JUDGMENT, HEAVEN, AND HELL   163

CHAPTER 10: SEEING THE INVISIBLE   186

The Invisible World

THE HAUNT DETECTOR

Everybody has one. The Reverend Frank Pavone used to call it *the Haunt Detector*. What is it?

Very simply, it's the little alarm that goes off in our heads whenever we detect that something mysterious or supernatural has occurred. Science fiction and horror writers have referred to it by other names—the *sixth sense*, the *shining*. But for some reason, I've always liked "haunt detector" best.

We actually have all kinds of "detecting" mechanisms built into our nervous systems. They don't have fancy scientific names, but they exist nonetheless. For instance, we all have "lie detectors." When someone who's not very slick tries to scam us, we're usually able to tell just from their body language and their voice. We all have "love detectors." We can just feel it in our bones when someone has deep feelings of attachment for us— or when they don't. We all have "right and wrong" detectors— better known as consciences. When we do something not quite right, we know it because we feel an unmistakable pang of guilt. And, of course, we all have "sex detectors," which let us know pretty quickly when we're physically attracted to another person.

Well, we all have "haunt detectors," too. And they let us know whenever something especially eerie or out of the ordinary is happening around us. You know the kind of thing. You could be sitting around relaxing one day at home, and for no special rea-son you start thinking about someone. Maybe you haven't thought about this particular person in years. Then the phone rings; you pick it up, and, amazingly, it's *that* person! Many of us have experienced this phenomenon. What is it?

I'll never forget something that happened to my mother many years ago. It was the middle of the night and she was sleeping soundly. Suddenly she woke up and bolted upright in bed. She had heard the sound of her own mother's voice calling out to her in a thick Italian accent: "Laura, Laura, help me." My mother was startled and her heart was racing; she had clearly heard her name spoken. But it couldn't be her mother calling; she lived on the other side of Brooklyn, and it was so late. My mother thought that perhaps it was just a bad dream so she went back to sleep. But the next morning she received a phone call from the hospital. Her mother had gotten up to go to the bathroom during the night and had fallen. She was in the hospital with a broken hip. For hours she had been on the floor, moaning for help. How in the world did my mother hear her? Was it just a coincidence?

Then there are stories that are totally unexplainable. I read a newspaper account a few years ago about a four-year-old girl in upstate New York who had been diagnosed with a brain tumor. The whole community had been praying fervently for her. All the churches in the neighborhood—Lutheran, Evangelical, Catholic—were all united in prayer that a miracle would take place. The little girl had been through so much: she'd had more than twenty MRIs, and it was decided that the only remaining course of action was brain surgery. She wasn't even expected to make it through the operation, but it was the only chance she had. The day of the surgery her head was shaved, her blood was taken, she was hooked up to all kinds of machines, and the team of doctors scrubbed and put on their surgical gowns. One final MRI had to be done to determine the exact location of the tumor. Just before the child was wheeled into the testing room, a sweet, pretty young nurse came in and took her hand. She told the little girl not to worry because she was "all better," that God had "cured" her and that she would be going home soon. The little girl later said that the nurse was so nice to her and so "beautiful" that she felt all warm and peaceful inside.

When the MRI was taken, the lab technicians gasped in disbelief. No matter how hard they searched, they couldn't locate the tumor. They took more tests, but the results were the same. The tumor was gone. No surgery was performed that day—or any day—because there was nothing to operate on. The little girl was completely healed. What happened? And who was the mysterious woman who came in and told the girl she was cured? None of the other nurses could identify her and no one ever saw her again. Was she an angel, as some in the little girl's family believed? No one knows for sure. But everyone, from the doctors to the lab technicians to the parents to the people in the community, was aware that something incredible had taken place. Everyone's haunt detectors went off at once.

Of course, not all mysterious experiences are as strange as this. A person's haunt detector can begin registering at any time. You can be listening to a powerful piece of music or watching a spectacular sunset; reading a particularly moving piece of literature or worshipping at church. You can be embracing the person you love most in the world or sitting in your home, cozy and warm by the fire. Or you can just be walking down the street thinking about all the things in your life that have brought you to where you are. You can be doing any of these things, and out of nowhere a tingle will suddenly run up your spine, telling you that something more is going on than meets the eye. Something that transcends understanding.

What is it? No one really knows. But it invariably triggers a feeling deep in your soul—a feeling of desire, of yearning, of hope; hope that there *is* something special about life; that there is some hidden meaning and purpose to all the suffering we have to go through; that there is something beyond science, beyond the senses—something totally invisible yet totally real. In Latin, the experience is called *mysterium tremendum et fascinans.* And our haunt detectors can sense it.

Of course, we have to be careful when trying to discern the meaning of such feelings and phenomena. Spiritual people are sometimes too quick to attribute the cause of strange occurrences to God; they're too hasty in coming to the conclusion that just because something seems unexplainable it must have a divine or supernatural origin. That simply isn't the case. Many amazing things that happen in this world aren't "miraculous" at all. It's a fact, for example, that human beings have all kinds of natural abilities that are untapped; abilities that are only now being identified and studied by science. We've all heard about mothers and fathers who display superhuman strength when trying to rescue their children from harm. We've all seen examples of people with severe learning disabilities who are able to sit down at a piano without any formal training and play the most complicated pieces of classical music. The human brain is an incredible organ and has many powers that still aren't fully understood. Because of this, it's extremely difficult for us to tell what's natural, what's supernatural, what's legitimately from God, what's from the devil, and what's just plain old human imagination. Practically everything that happens in life is subject to misinterpretation. That's why it's so dangerous to become fixated on the supernatural. Too often it leads to superstition or belief in the occult or false spirituality or even—in extreme cases—insanity.

We just can't afford to make blind assumptions. We have to seek the expert guidance of doctors, psychologists, scientists, theologians, and church leaders. But neither can we dismiss all these remarkable experiences as mere fantasy. And that's what many people do today. Not only do they reject what's fanciful and frivolous—they reject everything. They throw the baby out with the bathwater. They claim that there is no reality other than the reality of the senses, the reality of the material world. In many ways this is an even greater mistake. After all, it's one thing to be cautious and discerning when it comes to spiritual matters; it's quite another to deny the existence of the spiritual realm altogether.

If we do that, we risk falling into what has been called the "superstition of materialism," the myth that this world is made up of physical objects and nothing else; that everything in life—our thoughts, our emotions, our hopes, our ambitions, our passions, our memories, our philosophies, our politics, our beliefs in God and salvation and damnation—that all of this is purely the result of biochemical reactions and the movement of molecules in our brain. What nonsense!

We can't reduce the whole of reality to what our senses tell us for the simple reason that our senses are notorious for lying to us. Our senses tell us that the world is flat, yet it's not. Our senses tell us that the world is chaotic, yet we know that on both a micro and a macro level, it's incredibly organized. Our senses tell us that we're stationary, yet we're really moving at dizzying speeds. Right now, for instance, you're sitting down quietly reading this book; but did you know that you're actually traveling at twenty thousand miles per hour? That's the rate at which the earth and the entire galaxy are racing through space. Can you feel or see that motion in any way? Of course not. It's completely invisible to your senses. In fact, the only reason that you're not physically hurled into orbit right now is because another invisible force—gravity—is holding you in place. There are all kinds of unseen forces and laws that govern the universe. They're all invisible—and they're all very real.

The most important things in life can't be seen with the eyes. Ideas can't be seen. Love can't be seen. Honor can't be seen. This isn't a new concept. Judaism and Christianity and Islam and Buddhism and Taoism have all taught for thousands of years that the highest forms of reality are invisible. God is invisible, and he created the universe. Our souls are invisible, and they give life to our bodies. Angels are invisible, and they're the most powerful of God's creatures.

Are these unseen realities difficult for us to grasp? Of course. When the alarm clock goes off in the morning and we stumble out of bed to shower and dress and go to work, it's hard for us to focus on anything so intangible as the spiritual realm. After all, how can we hope to find an invisible God when we sometimes have trouble finding the milk in the refrigerator when it's staring us right in the face? C. S. Lewis said that human beings find it almost impossible to "believe in the unfamiliar while the familiar is before their eyes." One of the great psychological obstacles to having a strong faith is the very "ordinariness" of life.

In the first chapter of *The Screwtape Letters*, Lewis writes about the diabolical strategy that an invisible demon uses on an old, hardened atheist. The atheist, for the first time in his life, is starting to ask himself questions about the existence of God. The demon naturally wants to prevent this. But rather than waste his time arguing with the man about theology, the demon plants the suggestion in the atheist's mind to go out and have some lunch. Once in the street, the atheist sees the newspaper boy and the taxis going by and a thousand other small details. With that healthy dose of "real life" he doesn't even bother continuing his search for God. After all, in light of all those clear, crisp, ordinary realities, how could there be any such nebulous thing as metaphysical truth?

We face the same danger. Because we're so familiar with desks and chairs and pots and pans and cell phones and video games, it can be a real challenge for us to think about spiritual matters. Our haunt detectors can become so dulled and rusty from disuse that they hardly register any kind of invisible activity except the most extraordinary. The end result is that, although we may not become full-fledged atheists, we can actually begin *behaving* as if we were. Without even realizing it, a giant gap can form between what we profess to believe and how we go about acting in our everyday lives.

We all know how true this is. We say we believe in the Bible and the moral law, but then we have trouble going even a few weeks without breaking most of the Ten Commandments. We say we believe in the power of prayer and God's grace, but few of us actually turn to God unless we're in some sort of a jam. We act this way partly because of human nature. But it's also because the temptations we face seem so real, while the world of the spirit seems so hazy and unreal by comparison. In this hedonistic society of ours, in which we're confronted every day by thousands of images designed to appeal to our sensual appetites, it's very easy to be seduced. When a woman who loves chocolate passes a Godiva shop and sees a window full of delicious truffles, caramels, and other assorted treats, it's hard for her to consider the spiritual value of fasting or the Christian belief that the body is the "temple of the Holy Spirit." When a man with a healthy libido strolls down the streets of lower Manhattan on a sultry summer afternoon and is confronted by a parade of sexy, scantily clad women, it's tough for him to think about formless beings like angels. What are visible to him at that moment—the shapely forms enticing his senses—are just too much for him to resist. The spiritual world doesn't seem to stand a chance.

And that's where this book comes in. What I'd like to do in the following pages is attempt to render that spiritual world a bit more clearly for you. I'd like to try to make the invisible realities that surround us just a little more visible. My hope is that, by doing this, these realities won't seem so unfamiliar in the future. And the more familiar they are, the easier it will be to understand them and to have absolute faith in their existence. Once you're armed with that kind of certitude, three things will naturally happen: (1) It will be easier for you to act in sync with your moral beliefs; (2) your life will be much fuller, richer, and more exciting than you ever imagined possible; and (3) no amount of suffering—physical, mental, or emotional—will ever be able to destroy the profound inner sense of peace that you'll experience on a daily basis.

Big promises, I know. But that's how important this subject is.

So how does one go about making the invisible visible? Well, as I said, there's an extraordinarily rich theology from which we can draw. The traditional Judeo-Christian view of the invisible world has been largely displaced by a kind of fortune cookie philosophy of life that's neither truly believable nor truly remarkable. Just browse through the New Age section of your local bookstore and you'll see what I mean. This book is not going to be like that. It's not going to be about vampires or gremlins or ghosts or leprechauns or psychics or poltergeists or palm readers or UFOs or fairies or the "Force." This book is about reality—cold, hard reality.

In fact, one of the great things about the invisible realm is that you don't have to be a "religious fanatic" or the follower of some cult to believe in it. You can be a level-headed pragmatist. You can be a realist. You can even be a cynic. You certainly don't have to check your brains at the door before entering this world. And you don't have to be afraid that deep thinking is going to nullify what you learn there. Indeed, everything we're going to talk about in this book is based on solid theology, informed by common sense and logic, and backed up by biblical scholarship and the universal teaching of the Christian church over the past two thousand years.

No less a genius than Albert Einstein once said: "The most beautiful thing we can experience in life is the *mysterious*. It is the source of all true art and science. He to whom this emotion is a stranger, who can no longer pause to wonder and stand rapt in awe, is as good as dead: for his eyes are closed."

Too many people go through life today with their eyes closed. They miss out on the mysterious because they're so fixated on what they can see and smell and touch and taste and hear. They're so steeped in the "superstition of materialism" that they're totally blind to the existence of another world—a world that is radically different from the one they're familiar with, but a world nonetheless.

What kind of world is it? I've said that this book is not about make-believe; it's not going to be some kind of Peter Pan–style fairy tale. Yet I'd be lying if I didn't tell you that the hidden world God has created for us is more marvelous and exciting than a thousand Neverlands. It's a world filled with miracles, a world in which all the actions you take and decisions you make have spiritual consequences—consequences that affect the lives of millions of human beings. A world in which the men and women you meet on the street are never "ordinary"—because they all have immortal, everlasting souls and are destined to be either saints in Heaven or the damned of hell. A world in which a deadly, invisible, and diabolical war has been raging for eons—a war infinitely more terrifying than any started by Hitler, Stalin, or Osama bin Laden. A world where the highest values are completely opposite those of our secular society—where weakness equals strength, sacrifice equals salvation, and suffering equals unlimited power. Finally, it's a world in which you're never really alone, for even when you're by yourself watching TV or reading a book, taking a walk or sitting at the table having breakfast, you have company—because you're surrounded by angels.

Let's try for a few minutes to "see" this incredible world. Not with the eyes in your head, but with the eyes in your soul. All you really have to do is take a deep breath, shake off the stresses and cares that normally consume you, find a place where you can concentrate in quiet stillness, and do your best to keep an open mind. For just a little while, follow the biblical injunction to "walk by faith and not by sight."

And if—as you're reading—you happen to feel a tingle up your spine or experience the eerie sensation that something beyond your comprehension is taking place, don't get alarmed. It's just your haunt detector going off—telling you that the veil that has covered God's hidden creation from time immemorial is being pulled back ever so slightly, allowing you a chance to peek inside.

Don't be afraid to look. Believe me—you'll be amazed by what you see.

CHAPTER 2

THE INVISIBLE GOD

I don't know about you, but I've always had a tough time thinking about God. I've never known whether to picture him with
the face of a benevolent old man, as Michelangelo painted him
on the ceiling of the Sistine Chapel, or as a dazzling white light,
with hundreds of warm rays streaming from the center of his
formless Being, as he's been described by some who have had
near death experiences. Yes, I know that God is really neither of
these things, but it helps to have a concrete image in your head,
especially when you're praying.

I've also had trouble coming to grips with God's seemingly
paradoxical "personality." Maybe you can relate. On the one
hand, we've been taught to think of God simply as our "Father,"
as the one who created us and loves us. Indeed, we've heard over
and over again that God is Love and God is Mercy. The Bible
clearly says that human beings were made in the "image and
likeness" of God. Therefore he *must* be a Being very much like
us. He must be a Being we can understand and relate to, at least
on some level. Conceived in this way, God can be extremely
approachable. After all, what's more natural than speaking to
someone you have a lot in common with—or someone who loves
you?

But there's another way of looking at God. It's not as intimate, and not as comforting—but it is equally valid. It's possible to think of God as a Being who is so far *above* us as to be almost unfathomable and incomprehensible; as an entity so almighty, so all-knowing, and so totally different from us that it's almost absurd to even try to understand his complexities.

Indeed, when you consider the amazing powers that are commonly attributed to God, as compared with the ridiculously limited and feeble abilities of human beings, it's hard to imagine a greater contrast. It's hard to imagine how we can even hope to grasp—with our tiny intellects—something as sublime and infinite as the mind of God.

There's a wonderful story about Saint Augustine that illustrates this point well. The famous bishop of Hippo lived just before the fall of the Roman Empire. Today he's considered one of the Fathers of the Christian Church. One day he was working on a book about the nature of God and was meditating on one of the greatest mysteries in all theology, namely, that God is a "trinity" of "persons"—Father, Son, and Holy Spirit—and yet just one God.

Talk about a mystery! How can anything be three and one at the same time? Augustine racked his brains and pulled out his hair trying to make sense of this—but no matter how hard he tried, he couldn't get anywhere. So he did what a lot of us do when we have a problem we can't solve—he decided to take a break. He decided to leave his dark, cramped room and clear his head by taking a walk on the beach, which happened to be just a short distance from his home.

But as Augustine strolled along the shoreline, occasionally gazing out at the immense ocean, he continued trying to figure out the mystery. How could God be three distinct entities yet only one? He looked up to the clear blue sky above him and prayed: "God, help me to understand you!"

Feeling somewhat better but still frustrated, Augustine breathed in the good salt air and kicked up the sand in front of him. Just then he saw a little boy in the distance, running back and forth to the water. He was intrigued by the boy, who seemed to be engaged in a very serious game.

The little boy had dug a hole in the sand a few feet from where the surf was breaking. Augustine saw that the boy would run frantically to the water, scoop some up in his hands, run back to the sand, and promptly pour the water into the hole he had dug. Then he would turn around, go back to the ocean, and do the very same thing again.

What could this crazy boy be doing? wondered Augustine. By this time, he had stopped walking and was only a few feet from the child. But the boy took no notice of him and continued running back and forth to the hole. Finally, Augustine could contain himself no longer and said: "Little boy, what in the world are you doing?" The boy smiled and responded, "Well, sir, I've dug this hole here, and I'm trying to fill it up with all the water in the ocean." Augustine let out a hearty laugh, and said, "Boy, don't you know that you can't possibly fit the vast ocean into that tiny little hole!"

Then the boy stopped, looked directly into Augustine's eyes, and said very slowly and clearly in his little boy's voice: "And neither can you, Augustine, fit the vastness of God into your tiny little mind."

And with that the boy suddenly disappeared. Augustine

looked all around for him, but he was nowhere to be seen. He had vanished into thin air.

Now whether or not this story is true or just a legend isn't that important—there's a lot we can learn from it. For despite the fact that God is our "friend" and our "father," he's also as different from us as we are from the amoebas and the insects. No matter how smart we are or how much we study the Scriptures and theology, there's a very definite limit to what we can "know" about God. In fact, God is so different from us that theologians have sometimes referred to him with the strange title "totally other."

Totally other. This may seem a rather cold way of referring to God—and one that doesn't inspire much trust or affection—but there's a strong argument to be made that we really need to focus more on this "strangeness" and "otherness" of God—especially at this time in history. For we live in a very informal age—an age of extreme "familiarity." Indeed, nothing in our society is unfamiliar to us anymore. As a people we've grown so smart and smug. It's not so much that we're more intelligent than those who lived before us—we're not—it's that we *think* we have access, through technology and the Internet, to all human knowledge, indeed, to most (if not all) of the secrets of the universe.

The problem is that the old cliché about familiarity breeding contempt is just as valid when we apply it to God. We've all heard the complaint that "nothing is sacred anymore." In past decades this may have been an exaggeration. But what reasonable person could possibly deny its truth today? What reasonable person could possibly deny that God is more maligned and mocked now than at any time in recent history?

Bear in mind I'm not talking about Christians. I'm talking about God himself. Just spend a few minutes listening to the radio or watching TV. Hardly an hour will go by without God's name being "taken in vain." And that's the least of the offenses. Nothing pertaining to God—not faith, not the Bible, not the Church—is safe from frequent and venomous verbal assaults. The truth is that God just isn't given the respect today that he once was accorded—by either believers or nonbelievers.

Of course, there are many reasons for this—it's not just simple "familiarity." One obvious cause is that we've become a much more secular and atheistic society and just don't care as much about God and all his "rules." Another is that there really is a spiritual battle going on between the forces that are aligned with God and the invisible "powers and principalities" that Saint Paul spoke so famously about. That's a subject we'll come back to later on.

But for now it's important to understand that *because* God is so ignored and disrespected today, it's more critical than ever before that we reflect on those qualities of his that are *not* so familiar to us. It's more critical than ever before that we think about those divine attributes that inspire in us not only a feeling of love but a feeling of awe. It's more critical than ever before that we discuss what is unfathomable and incomprehensible about God—and not dwell exclusively on the fact that he is so close to us.

And what are these incomprehensible qualities of God?

The most obvious is that he's invisible. He is totally undetectable, unobservable, and imperceptible to our senses. Think about that for a moment. God exists; he's real, and he's busy doing all kinds of extraordinary things, but he's cloaked in an impenetrable veil of invisibility.

Back when I was first beginning to believe in God, I used to have a big problem with this. What was the point of God being invisible? I thought. Was this some kind of game he was playing with us? Some kind of silly, cosmic version of hide-and-seek? If God really existed—which I highly doubted—why in the world would he feel the need to be hidden from the very creatures he created? I just didn't get it. In the books I read that argued the pros and cons of the existence of God, everyone seemed to be so concerned with the problem of suffering. That, apparently, was the main reason people didn't believe in a personal God. But I hadn't even gotten to the time in my life where suffering was a significant factor (that would come later). I was stuck at a completely different point. I just couldn't get past the fact that God had supposedly created this beautiful three-dimensional Technicolor world, and then made what was, to me, an arbitrary decision to remain totally colorless, formless, and unseen. It just didn't make sense.

Then it dawned on me that perhaps I was being unfair to God. Maybe he hadn't made an "arbitrary" decision to be invisible to us. Maybe God was invisible for the simple reason that he was spirit, and that's what spirits are—invisible. The fact that we can't see God the way we see a book or a cell phone or the person standing in front of us isn't because God *wants* to be hidden from us. It's that it is his *nature* to be hidden from us. In other words, when God created the universe, he created something radically new and different from himself. The material realm of the senses is completely unlike the extrasensory, supernatural realm of the spiritual. One is, intrinsically, visible, and the other is, intrinsically, invisible. Period. So maybe the fact that we couldn't see God wasn't because he was playing any kind of game with us. Maybe he was just being extremely creative.

Now, of course, God did make a decision, *indirectly*, to be invisible. He knew from the start that if he invented physical creatures with physical eyes, they wouldn't have the ability to see invisible spirits. Yet he went ahead with his plan for creation anyway. Why?

One very basic reason is that God didn't want to allow human beings to be able to place him "in a box." I mentioned before that we've grown so snobbish that we think we can measure, analyze, and experiment on anything we want today, including God. And that attitude, I'm afraid, just doesn't cut it with the Almighty.

Case in point: I recently saw a study in the news dealing with the effectiveness of prayer. In this experiment, researchers attempted to "test" whether prayer "works" by measuring the effect it had on people with different kinds of diseases or medical ailments. Aside from the preposterousness of the test variables (how in the world can you measure whether the prayers being said were sincere or insincere?), the whole premise of the experiment was flawed because of the biblical assurance we have from God that he absolutely refuses to be "put to the test." For if there really is a God, he isn't going to sit back and allow the creatures he made to cavalierly put him under a microscope and subject him to their little experiments—as if he were some kind of a high school science project!

And the truth is that if God were not invisible, this inclination of ours to treat him with the same condescending coldness with which we treat other material objects would be even more pronounced. If we could plainly see God in the sky—let's say, somewhere up to the left, and just below the moon—we would automatically think of him as something that was limited and finite, instead of something unlimited and infinite. We would have even more of a tendency to view him as a scientific specimen that we could dissect and classify—instead of an awesome Being whom we should love and worship.

God knew this from the beginning. He knew that if he were visible to us, we couldn't help but feel "superior" to him in some way—or at least equal; that we couldn't help but want to put him in a box. And he just wasn't going to permit it. He wasn't going to let us short-circuit the method that he himself had ordained from time immemorial as the proper way of seeking him. You see, what God wants most from us is that we come to know him *not* through rigorous scientific proof—but through simple faith and trust.

And isn't that something we can all understand? Isn't that something that we ourselves expect from the people with whom we want to have relationships? How would you like it if someone you considered a friend said to you, "I want to continue knowing you, but I'm afraid I can't until I see with my own eyes some compelling proof that you're my friend"?

Don't we demand from our own family and friends that they trust us *first*, without requiring some kind of demonstrable evidence of our loyalty? And don't we have the greatest affection for those special people in our lives who love us and trust us and have faith in us even when it's not so apparent how wonderful we are? Well, why should it be any different with God? Why should he want a relationship with us founded on anything but trust?

If God were clearly visible in the sky, he would basically be *forcing* us to acknowledge him. And he doesn't want that. He doesn't want us to either condescendingly put him in a box or be so awed by the sight of him that we feel we *must* listen to him. He doesn't want to compel us to believe in him either by showing his face plainly, or by forcing our minds to accept him through conclusive, irrefutable logic. If there's one thing to understand about God, it's that he doesn't want to force us to do *anything*.

God wants us to trust him of our own free will. He wants us to say: "I can't see you, Lord, but I have faith in you and will listen to you because of everything you've said and done in the past; because of everything you're doing right now; and because you've shown by your wondrous actions that you are deserving of my trust—even though I can't prove it with mathematical certitude."

That's the kind of affirmation God wants from us. The challenge is that in order to affirm God in this manner, it helps to have some sense of wonder about him. And as we just discussed a few pages ago, a sense of wonder is exactly what we in the cynical twenty-first century have lost.

Can we retrieve it? Yes! But in order to do so, we have to take some time to remind ourselves how truly amazing this God of ours is. We have to remember that God is much more than just an invisible spirit. He is also a Being who is *all-powerful*. We've heard this phrase bandied about before, but we rarely give it much thought. After all, when was the last time you thought about what it means for God to have the ability to create something out of nothing? If you closed your eyes now and used all your powers of concentration, could you create anything—even the smallest pebble? And yet God created the universe just by "speaking" a word. He didn't roll up his sleeves or hire any construction workers or use any tools. Essentially, he thought it, and it was there. *That's* how God makes things—by conceiving them in his "mind" and willing them into existence.

Now imagine the power of a star; imagine the power of the trillions of hydrogen explosions that take place on the surface of all the stars in the galaxy; imagine the planets, the comets, the asteroids, the quasars, the pulsars, the black holes, and the dark void of space itself. Imagine the vastness of the whole universe, and then remember that God simply "thought" it and "spoke" a word, and by the power of his will it all came into being out of nothing.

God also *maintains* everything in existence. Creation is not just a "one-time" deal for him. Because God "thinks" things into being, he must continue to think about them; otherwise they would go out of existence. The process is similar to the way ideas come and go in our own minds. The moment we cease thinking about a particular thought, it's no longer there—it pops out of our head and out of existence until the next time we think about it. It's the same with God. If he stopped thinking about the universe, the universe itself would go out of existence. If he stopped thinking about *you* for just one second, *you* would go out of existence. What this means is that, at every moment of the day and every moment of the night, God is busy "focusing" on you. He created you, but he didn't stop there and "go on to the next person." His mind continues to concentrate on you, like a high-powered laser beam, even when you're sleeping. This is one of the reasons that the great religions of the world have always taught that we shouldn't spend so much time thinking about ourselves. We don't have to be self-centered, because God is already doing that for us.

It follows that since God made everything and maintains everything, he therefore *knows* everything. All the sciences, from physics to biology to chemistry to geology to astronomy, are merely attempts to put into human language things that God has invented. Think of Einstein's mathematical formulas, think of the physical laws that govern the universe, think of all the natural wonders of the earth, think of the vast amount of knowledge and information contained in all the libraries, all the universities, and all the computers of the world, and then realize that God knows all of it, down to the tiniest detail.

Consider the implications. If God is all-knowing, he knows everything about *you*, too. For not only did he create you, but he also planned you, from all eternity. Before Columbus discovered America—before there even was an America—God knew your name and everything about you, from your height to your weight to the color of your eyes to your favorite food. God knows you better than you know yourself. He knows your faults, your strengths, your weaknesses, your full potential, and all your deep, dark secrets. God knows what you're thinking right this second, and he knows what you'll be thinking an hour from now. There is *nothing* you know about yourself that God does not know better. And there are thousands of things you don't realize about yourself that God is intimately aware of.

Finally, God has no beginning and no end. There never was a time when God did not exist—and there never will be. Time, itself, was created by God when he made the material universe. In some special, mysterious way, time exists *inside* God. Because of this, God has no past and no future. For God, everything is the present. That's why God is able to see all of history in one glance. He sees the Big Bang and he sees the dinosaurs and he sees you reading this book, all at the same time. God is able to see all of your history in one glance, too. When God looks down from Heaven and observes what you're doing *right now*—he sees you reading these words with the exact same clarity that he sees you as a baby being born in the hospital—*right now*—and with the exact same clarity that he sees you as an elderly person taking your last breath on your deathbed—*right now*. He sees all the times of your life in the present moment, on the same timeless page with the same timeless eyes.

These are just a few of God's powers. There are many more. Each could be the subject of its own book, and each amply demonstrates not only how superior God is to his creatures, but also how "totally other" he is.

There's a story I like that illustrates this point. It concerns one of the most famous Christian thinkers of all time, Thomas Aquinas. Aquinas was an immensely influential philosopher and theologian who lived during the thirteenth century. He's perhaps best known for his "five ways" of demonstrating God's existence. But he did incredibly brilliant work in almost every field—law, ethics, logic, Christian apologetics, philosophy, and theology. He's also the author of the monumental *Summa Theo-logica*, and the man who, when asked what he was most grateful to God for, responded: "that I have understood every page I have ever read."

One day, for no apparent reason, this great defender of the faith suddenly stopped working. He just stopped cold. He was in the middle of one of his huge projects, and he practically broke off in the middle of a sentence. And he never wrote another word. Why? Because he had an extraordinary encounter with God.

The story goes that one afternoon he was praying intently, his mind deep in contemplation. All of a sudden, he had a vision. Not just any vision. A vision of God. In one moment—and it lasted for only a moment—God showed himself to Aquinas. Aquinas didn't see God "face-to-face," as we're destined to see him in Heaven; but in some mysterious way, God showed Aquinas a "glimpse" of himself. And Aquinas was paralyzed. He was literally frozen on the spot where he had been praying. And as he experienced this ecstasy, he heard a voice say to him: *"Thomas, thou hast written well of me."*

He was overcome. In fact, for days afterward he wasn't able to say or do anything. He didn't eat. He didn't sleep. He didn't write. Finally, one of his friends begged him to tell him what had happened; he begged Aquinas to rouse himself out of his daze and continue his important writing. Aquinas finally looked at him and said in a solemn voice: "I can do no more. Such secrets have been revealed to me that all I have written seems to me like straw." And he never picked up a pen again.

That's what the experience of just glimpsing God did to one of the greatest minds of all time.

And yet despite the truth of all this—despite the truth of how wondrous and awesome and "totally other" God is—I would be lying if I didn't admit that it can sometimes be difficult to feel connected to this amazing Being we can't see or touch. It can be hard to pray, year in and year out, to an entity more formless and colorless than a wisp of smoke. No matter how accurate it is to say that we owe God the full measure of our devotion, the fact is that his invisibility *is* a stumbling block to us.

And this is the great catch-22 of faith. God is invisible because he wants us to believe in him without being coerced; but at the same time he understands how weak we are and how psychologically dependent we are on our senses. He wants us to have faith in something we can't see or touch, yet he knows how much we desperately want to see, touch, hear, and smell everything—and he's sympathetic to us. The question is: how can we escape from this endless loop? Is there a way for humans to satisfy God's "faith test" and also have something tangible to grab on to? Is there a way, in other words, for us to have our cake and eat it, too?

And the answer is yes, there is. There is a solution to the problem—and God has found it. Somehow he has devised a way to be both seen and unseen at the same time. In fact, his solution was so original and surprising that only God himself could have come up with it. Two thousand years ago, God decided to become visible—every bit as visible as you and I and the grocer next door. But he did it in a way that would not allow us to "put him in a box," in a way that was not so overwhelming that we would be forced to bow down and worship at his feet, and in a way that still requires us to have faith in him. God's solution to the great catch-22 of faith was *Christmas*.

Christmas (along with the Annunciation) is the celebration of the Incarnation—the mystery of God becoming man. And on that first Christmas Eve in Bethlehem, so many years ago, that's exactly what happened. The intangible God of Abraham and Moses finally became tangible. The eternal, infinite God, who fills every part of the universe, finally became a finite person. The unseen Creator of the world at long last became visible to the world; with eyes and ears and a nose and a face.

And it was the face of a little baby.

The miracle of Christmas is that the child crying in the straw-filled manger *is* God. The little hand that reached up to his mother from the cradle is the very same hand that steers the stars and planets in their orbits. The eyes of the baby that dimly perceived the animals kneeling in the dark stable are the very same eyes that see all of history in one glance. It is because of the power of *that* child that you and I are able to take our next breath.

What happened that first Christmas goes way beyond anything we can conceive of in our tiny intellects. God actually appeared at a specific time in human history, in a specific place, and with the cooperation of specific people. The great message of Christmas is that God himself has become specific.

No longer can anyone claim that God is something vague and cloudy—a nebulous, invisible spirit somewhere out there watching us "from a distance." From time immemorial, humanity has had questions about the unseen God: Who is he? Where is he? What does he look like? What does he really think of me? Is he on my side? Thanks to Christmas, we know the answers to those questions. God himself is no longer a question mark. For Jesus Christ is God in human language.

When we see Jesus, we see God. When we hear the words of Jesus, we hear the words of God—human words. And we know with absolute certitude that God is on our side. Why? Because of the man the child in the manger grew up to be; because of his preaching, because of the miracles he performed, because of the Church he founded, because of the fact that he was tortured and killed for our sake—all so that we could enjoy eternal life in heaven.

And while it's true that Christ is not visible today in the same way he was when he walked the streets of Palestine (he's in Heaven now, *with* his human body, which is something we'll talk about later), that doesn't take away from the fact that he did indeed walk among us at one time. Essentially, God came into our physical, material world because he knew how difficult it was for us to understand his own immaterial, spiritual world. He lowered himself to our level so that we could finally understand him on our terms. And even more important, he became a man so that he could raise us up *above* the world of matter and be caught up in the love of higher, invisible realities—the very realities we're going to discuss in this book.

It's no wonder Christmas is such a special holiday. Other religious celebrations may be more "important." Easter, for example, is the holiest day of the year, because it commemorates the most important event in history—the Resurrection of Christ and Redemption of Mankind. But there's something magical about Christmas. You don't have to be a child to know that it's more than just a holiday. It's a celebration of the deepest and most profound mystery of life—the mystery of the invisible becoming visible. And whether you're young or old, there's a certain undeniable thrill about this mystery that goes straight to the core of the human soul.

That's why it's so appropriate that the Christmas season is full of so many wonderful things—things that don't even have to do with the practice of religion: all the hustling and bustling, all the twinkling lights, all the brightly colored bows, all those delicious Christmas smells—the food cooking, the cinnamon, the holly, the pine needles, the roasting chestnuts—the wonderfully gaudy, happy Christmas trees, the bright red poinsettias, the big green wreaths, the sparkling golden garland, the family gathering together, the excited children; and most of all, the feeling of anticipation—anticipation of presents, of people, of laughter. All of these things, together, create an atmosphere of magic; they convey the sensation that something different is going on here, something strange and wonderful, something *totally other*.

And that's the key. Christmas is wondrous because it somehow captures the paradoxical nature of God that we've been speaking about. We said earlier that God is a Being who is so far above us that he's almost unfathomable and incomprehensible; yet he's also someone we can relate to on the most intimate terms. We said that he's all-powerful and all-knowing, yet he's also all-loving and all-good. We said that his nature is to be completely invisible to our senses, yet he chose to become visible despite that nature. Christmas is really the focal point in time and space, because it represents the convergence of these paradoxes, the point at which the material and spiritual dimensions of the world meet.

The question that remains is, why? Why would God want to become human? If he's really as far above us as we are above the insects and the amoebas, what could he possibly gain by lowering himself to such an extraordinary degree? Yes, we know that the Incarnation helped *us*, but what was in it for *him*? Can you imagine ever choosing to become a microbe, even if you absolutely loved the study of biology? Can you imagine ever becoming an ant, even if you were particularly fond of insects? Of course not! The very thought is inconceivable. Then what in the world could have motivated God?

That's a question, I'm afraid, that we won't be able to answer till the end of this book, because it involves many other subjects—including the relationship between humility and happiness, the true meaning of love, and what our life will be like in Heaven. For the moment, let's stop here. Let's resist the urge to be like Saint Augustine and try to put the "vastness of God" into our tiny little minds. Instead, let's turn our attention to another spiritual reality—one that is, in many ways, the most fascinating of all because it was the very *first* of God's invisible creations.

I'm talking about the very real—but very mysterious—world of the angels.

CHAPTER 3

INVISIBLE HELPERS

The World of the Angels

In his book *Angels: God's Secret Agents*, Billy Graham relates an amazing incident involving the Reverend John G. Paton, a nineteenth-century Scottish missionary in the remote New Hebrides Islands in the South Pacific.

Living on the island of Tanna with his wife, the Reverend Paton did his best to minister to the needs of the natives—a task that proved both difficult and dangerous. Not only did the half-savage and often cruel inhabitants of the region resist the efforts of the missionaries, but they often made war on them. Many times the missionaries ended up not serving, but *being served* as the main entrée at the village luau! For the natives of the New Hebrides were cannibals.

One evening Rev. Paton and his wife discovered to their horror that their hut was surrounded by an armed, hostile tribe of warriors, shouting angry threats and beating their war drums. It was clear they were getting ready to attack. Realizing that their lives were at an end and that they would soon be slaughtered and eaten, the couple began praying fervently to God. An hour went by, then two hours, then three, then five, and no attack came. Rev. Paton and his wife continued to pray the entire night. Early the next morning they opened the door of their hut and looked outside, and all the natives were gone.

Why had they left? It was a mystery.

Over the next two years Rev. Paton and his missionaries were left to do their work in peace. No more attacks were made on his little community. Soon his efforts began to bear fruit, and within a short time most of the native population of New Hebrides was converted to Christianity.

It was after this conversion that Rev. Paton finally met— face-to-face—the chief of the cannibal warriors who had once been so hostile to him and his missionaries. With some trepidation Rev. Paton asked the chief about that terrifying night years earlier when the chief's tribe had appeared ready to kill him and his wife. "Why didn't you attack?" he asked.

The chief looked at Rev. Paton with deep respect and said that he had indeed intended to slaughter him and his wife, but that his men had stopped when they saw "a hundred soldiers with shining garments, armed with sharp swords, surrounding the hut." These mysterious soldiers said nothing. They just stood there, motionless, illuminating the dark night with their glowing white garments. Rev. Paton questioned the chief intently, asking whether or not he could have been mistaken, but the chief was absolutely certain of what he had witnessed. It was the sight of those strange, ghostly soldiers guarding the hut that had petrified his men and caused them to flee in terror, resolving never to bother the missionaries again. Rev. Paton knew then that God had answered his prayers that night and sent an army of angels to protect him and his wife so that his mission to convert the natives could be accomplished.

This is only one of thousands of stories concerning the remarkable spiritual creatures we know as angels.

Who are the angels, really? What are they like, and what do they do? It seems that modern society is obsessed with them. Everywhere you look there are images of angels—angel books, angel poems, angel calendars, angel pictures, angel pins, angel ornaments, angel pillow cases, angel blankets, angel dolls, angel clocks, angel candles—even angel credit cards! There's a whole global industry devoted to these celestial beings.

And everywhere you turn, people seem to have angel stories, too. All you have to do is surf the Internet and you'll learn all about how an angel "saved my aunt Martha from being hit by a car," or "rescued my child from a burning building," or "introduced my brother to his wife," or "got me money to pay my mortgage." You'll read poignant and touching tales that have an unmistakable ring of authenticity—as well as stories that are almost impossible to take seriously, no matter how sincere and well meaning the writer. I saw one web page recently called "Amazing Angel Sightings" and read the following amusing titles: "Angels at the ATM," "The Angel and My Harley Davidson," "Wet and Wild Angel Story," and my favorite—"Pizza Dude Angel"!

What are we to make of all this? How can we separate the real from the phony, the authentically supernatural from the simply silly?

The answer is—we can't. The topic is just too subjective. And that's why we're not even going to try. As I said at the outset of this book, I'm not going to indulge in wild speculation or relate hundreds of personal anecdotes that may or may not be true. That's not to say that the stories people tell about angels aren't true. Some of them probably are—maybe even most of them. But this book has to stick to what's been revealed in Scripture and the authentic teaching of Christianity over twenty centuries. If we don't stay within these parameters, we're liable to drift into the worst kind of make-believe.

And there's no reason to do that. As is so often the case, the old, traditional truth about angels is much more fascinating than any fantasies concocted by human beings. And the simple reason is that God's imagination is a lot better than ours!

What *is* this truth about angels?

Well, first of all—they exist. They're real. They're not mythological creations or the stuff of fairy tales. They're as real as you and me. If you're going to get anything out of this chapter, please understand that. People everywhere seem to be fascinated by the *idea* of angels, but I don't think they take the concrete reality too seriously. They don't believe, in their heart of hearts, that angels are as real as they are—that they're alive, that they're all around us.

Yet that's a fact. Right now, as you are reading these words, there is an angel right next to you. I don't know if he's to your left or to your right, or if he's sitting or standing or hovering. Since he's a spirit, he's really not doing any of those things. He's just there. And there may be several other angels in the room with the two of you as well. In fact, there may be dozens. Sometimes—for instance, when you're with a group of people praying or when you're at church—there are hundreds, maybe even thousands, of angels present.

The reason that we need to be so clear about this is that

angels are not a small, unimportant part of Christianity. They're an essential part. And not only of Christianity, but of all the major religions of the world. Judaism, Islam, and Taoism all proclaim the existence of angels. These belief systems teach that God created the angels the same way he created the universe—out of nothing. They teach that angels are invisible spirits that were made by God either before or together with the material universe. They teach that although angels are invisible, God allows them—on certain very rare occasions—to manifest themselves to human beings in a visible way. They teach that angels have intellect and free will, and that when they were created, they were able to choose whether to serve God or turn against him. They teach that angels have spectacular powers that are cosmic in magnitude; that the number of angels is prodigious—in fact, they use words such as "armies," "legions," and "multitudes" to describe them. They teach that there seems to be, within these multitudes, a mysterious system of "ranking." Indeed, angels seem to live in a "society" of some kind. And finally, the major religions of the world teach that the primary thing that distinguishes angels from the rest of creation is that they are *pure spirits*.

This is an admittedly hard concept for us to grasp. Being a pure spirit means that you don't have a body. It means that you're invisible. It means that you're not bound by the limits of space—or by any of the limitations that matter imposes on us. Think about that for a moment. What are the limitations of matter?

Material objects and creatures have to be in one place at one time, and they can get to another place only if they physically move there—inch by inch, foot by foot, mile by mile—and this totally depends on their means of locomotion. In fact, every function performed by material creatures depends on their design and construction. The way they get their energy, the way they dispose of waste, the way they come to know things—it's all tied, in some way or other, to their bodies. Even the way they think and feel is "wired" through their nervous systems.

And, of course, material creatures deteriorate over time. They age. They get old and worn and lose their ability to function—and eventually, die.

Being a pure spirit means that you have none of these restrictions. It means that you're not bound by the constraints of physical space. You don't have to "move" in order to go somewhere else. You can just "be" wherever you want, whenever you want. It means that you don't have to think with the help of the brain; you don't have to depend on your senses to learn things, see things, smell things, or know things. And it means that you don't ever deteriorate. Being a pure spirit means, by definition, that you are immortal.

In practical terms, this means that angels are pretty extraordinary creatures. Rev. Paul O'Sullivan, in his book *All About the Angels*, says:

> *The intellect of an angel is incomparably superior to the human intellect. . . . The human mind has to plod from truth to truth just as the human body moves step by step, whereas the angelic intelligence grasps the whole of a subject at a single glance. Seeing a principle, it sees at once all its consequences, seeing a truth it sees at the same time all its possible aspects. . . . The*

movement of angels is marvelous, too. In a single instant, an angel comes from Heaven to Earth or goes from one end of the universe to the other without passing through the intermediate space. To understand this angelic movement, we have only to compare it with our thought. In a moment our thought passes from Heaven to Earth, from England to China, from end to end of the world. Angels are, if we might say so, living thoughts. . . .

Obviously, all of this is very difficult to comprehend. If you're a fish in the sea, it's hard to understand the life of a bird in the air. Pure spirits are just too radically different for us to grasp fully. In fact, the only reason that we *can* relate to the angels—at least a little bit—is because whereas they are pure spirits, we are *not* pure matter. Human beings are both body and spirit—we have something called a soul. In other words, we can understand spiritual matters in some way because we are part spirit.

And this is an interesting point. We said in the last chapter that God the Father is pure spirit. When he decided to start making things, he began with the angels—who are also pure spirits. In other words, his first creation resembled him the most—at least in terms of "substance." Then God decided to do something really different—he created the world of matter: the visible universe, the stars, the planets, the earth, the oceans, the mountains, and so on. Finally, he decided to combine the two—matter and spirit, body and soul. And that's what human beings are. Essentially, we're hybrids or, as C. S. Lewis referred to us, "amphibians."

Thus, God first created pure spirit, then pure matter, and finally, spirit-matter. When you think about it, it's amazing how organized he is!

It must have really been something to watch in the beginning when "God created the heavens and the earth." Can you visualize the scene? Remember, the angels had a front-row seat. One moment there was nothing. All was invisible. Then, a millisecond later, at the very instant God made his momentous decision and "spoke" his word of creation, the great void of invisible nothingness suddenly burst to life in a stupendous explosion of color and sound. The blinding light from millions of newly formed stars lit up the sky, and whole galaxies were hurled through space, zooming into vast, empty regions of the universe. And on one tiny planet, from the boiling quantum "soup" that eventually became its oceans, the building blocks of life came together, and living, breathing organisms began to emerge.

Yes, the angels were really treated to the most astonishing display of God's powers. No one knows what they thought at the time, or what their reaction to the grand spectacle was. All we know for sure is that, from the very start, God began using them in a special way; he began sending them on "missions" related to the newborn universe and its strange two-legged inhabitants—human beings.

What was the nature of these missions? Well, according to the Bible, there were many different kinds.

First and foremost, angels served as God's *messengers* to mankind. We see this throughout the Old and New Testaments, as God repeatedly used the angels to communicate his will to individuals such as Abraham, Moses, Jacob, Gideon, Daniel, the Virgin Mary, Zechariah, Joseph, and a whole host of saints and prophets. God also entrusted angels with the care of kingdoms and communities that were experiencing crisis, and in this capacity their primary mission was to defend, assist, and protect God's people (as in the incident of Rev. Paton and the cannibals). As Christians know, angels played a very important role in Christ's mission to save the world. Aside from announcing the good news to Mary, Joseph, and the shepherds, they also protected the newborn Jesus from the persecution of Herod. Later on, angels were present at the empty tomb when Jesus rose from the dead; later still, angels liberated the apostle Peter from prison when he was in danger of being executed.

Angels are characterized as "ministering spirits" in the Bible, and we see that they were often sent to give human beings consolation during periods of great suffering. The most touching example of this, perhaps, was when an angel was sent to the Garden of Gethsemane to comfort Jesus during his agony.

In the book of Revelation, we're told that angels will play a key role in the culmination of salvation history, when, at the end of time, they accompany Christ at his Second Coming—and then destroy the world. That's right. According to the Bible, angels will be the ones responsible for bringing ultimate destruction to planet Earth.

Of course, the best known mission of the angels is to be our *personal guardians*. Throughout sacred Scripture we find it implied that each of us has our own angel watching over us in a highly unique and personal manner. The purpose of this guardianship is very simple—to assist us to get to Heaven. Why would

God give these angels such a task? Basically because we need their help!

Remember, human beings have free will. We have the ability to make our own decisions. We're not computers. We're not programmed by God to act one way or another. Yes, there are plenty of forces that influence our actions and even seem to compel us to behave in certain ways—our genetics, our environment, our habits, and so on—but, ultimately, we have the power to act the way we want to act, to decide the way we want to decide. That's really what we mean when we say that we were made in the "image and likeness" of God. Like God, we have an intellect and free will. And like God, we have the power to create—not just art and music and other little humans—but to "create" ourselves, i.e., our identities.

The difficulty, as we all know, is that we don't always create ourselves in ways that we should. We don't always do what's right or what's best for us or even what we want to do. We don't always follow the road marked out for us by God—the road that leads to Heaven. And that's where our guardian angels come in. Their job is to help us get back onto the right road whenever they see us begin to stray off.

And they accomplish this mission by doing all the things we just listed a moment ago: by acting as messengers for God, by protecting us when God wants us protected, by playing unseen but pivotal roles at key moments in our lives, and by consoling us when we're going through great trials. In other words, they do all the things that angels have been doing for human beings throughout history, only they do them for us *personally.*

How do guardian angels go about their job? Well, obviously,

if the primary goal of these creatures is to influence our behavior in a positive way, then one of the things they have to do is *persuade* us to think and act in a manner that's beneficial to us. But since they can't talk to us the same way we talk to each other—with audible, physical sounds—they must necessarily communicate with us in a different way. They must communicate with our souls.

And this is exactly what our guardian angels do. They "talk" directly to the spiritual part of our nature. You see, in order for human beings to communicate, we need to channel everything through our brain and lungs and vocal cords and mouth. And not only that, we have to use words and language. Angels don't have to go that route. They can impress upon our minds and our souls a "thought" instantaneously, and completely bypass all the physical and linguistic channels.

Now, since we're so completely tied to our bodies, we still have to "process" these communications physiologically. That means that even when an angel "talks" to our soul, we still have to "listen" and "understand" with our bodies. There's just no way around it—everything has to go through the wiring of our brains and nervous systems. The result is that when our guardian angel tells us something, there are a variety of ways we can interpret the message physically.

Angels understand this. They understand everything about us, including the way our bodies handle different kinds of communications from them. And they take this knowledge into account when they talk to us. In fact, they vary the strength of their communications based on the way they know our bodies are going to react. Here are two examples of how this process might work in real-life "angelic" situations.

Let's say you're walking down a city street and see a beggar on the corner. Your guardian angel, who is at your side twenty-four hours a day, seven days a week, sees the beggar, too. Perhaps your intention is to walk quickly past the man without turning your head. Your angel, however, watching the situation and realizing this, decides to get involved. He decides to give you the inspiration to do a good deed.

Obviously this isn't a monumental event in your life. There's no need for any lightning and thunder from God. In fact, you might already be disposed to giving the beggar some money; it's just that you're in a bit of a rush and can't be bothered at the moment. In a situation like this, your angel doesn't have to do much. He just needs to give you a little nudge. So what he does is simply smuggle into your mind the idea that perhaps you should stop, reach into your pocket, and give the beggar some spare change or even a few dollars. It's just a tiny thought, and your brain has no problem processing it. In fact, to you it seems that the idea completely originated within yourself. At most, you might interpret the nudge as a slight pang of conscience. The result is that you stop and follow through on the inspiration. No one is ever the wiser, yet a kind act has been performed for the poor, and you have moved a small step closer to becoming the kind of creature God wants you to be.

Then there are those times when something enormously important might be at stake. Maybe even your life. You might be driving down a highway going quite fast, thinking about a problem at work or listening to music. Unknown to you, a few miles up the road and coming from the opposite direction is a big pickup truck whose driver has had much too much to drink. You have no way of knowing, but in a few minutes that drunk driver is going to lose control of his vehicle, jump the guardrail, and come barreling into you at eighty miles per hour. Meanwhile your two children are playing in the backseat of your car, and they're not wearing seat belts.

Well, it just so happens that it's *not* your time to die—or your children's. So your guardian angel, who sees all this and who has been told by God that he has permission to get involved, springs into action. Only this time, he can't take a chance on just "nudging" you. He can't simply inject a quiet little idea into your head. Too much is at stake, and there's no time to fool around. So your angel doesn't just "talk" to your mind; he communicates with real power. He screams right into your soul!

And what happens? All of a sudden you're jolted out of your daydreams. Your brain, for no apparent reason, along with your whole nervous system, sends a signal to your body, and every single muscle becomes as tense and taut as piano wire; you immediately stop listening to the music, and your mind focuses like a laser beam on one single thought—the safety of your children. Without knowing why, you practically yell to your kids, "Put those seat belts on *right now*."

Just a few seconds later, the accident foreseen by the angel occurs: the pickup truck jumps the divider and crashes into your car, which spins 360 degrees and smacks into the guardrail on the opposite side of the highway. The children are shaken and crying, both vehicles are totaled, there's shattered glass everywhere—but miraculously, no one is hurt. Everyone walks away, and you're left with your mouth open, wondering what just happened. For days and weeks afterward you ask yourself this question: "Why in the world did I tell my children to put their seat belts on at just that moment? Why did I suddenly feel the overwhelming compulsion to do that?"

Strange incidents like this occur all the time—"freak coincidences" that miraculously result in lives being saved. Sometimes angels are involved, and sometimes not. I'm afraid we'll never know for sure till we get to Heaven. The point is that these celestial creatures don't spend their time just sitting around playing their harps. They're frequently intervening in our lives, and they're doing so in ways that are both subtle and powerful. Sometimes they give commands as simple as "Look this way" or "Look that way." Sometimes they inject thoughts into our minds that inspire us to be better human beings. Sometimes they try to get us to avoid sinning by "nagging" at our consciences. Sometimes they tug at our heartstrings by reminding us of certain memories from our past in an attempt to make us reconcile with family members or friends with whom we've quarreled. Whatever the particular mission happens to be, they're always at our side, encouraging us, consoling us, coaching us, warning us, reminding us, and even yelling at us—all with one objective: to help us achieve the purpose for which we were created—to be in union with God both here on earth and for all eternity in Heaven.

And that's the key, I think, to understanding why angels have captivated our imagination in such a powerful way. Although they are pure spirits, we don't think of them as being "far away" or "up there, somewhere"—as we do other spiritual realities. While we understand that angels are always in Heaven with God, we also know that they're down here with us right now, getting their hands dirty in the nitty-gritty details of our daily existence. Angels are mysterious and strange and invisible, but they're also our fellow creatures—our half-brothers, you might say—and they're essentially living part of their lives on earth in order to help us. More than anything else, it's their proximity to us that's so intriguing.

In fact, angels are so close to us that it can be a little unsettling at times. If it's true that they're watching our every move, one question naturally arises: Is it possible to have any secrets from them? And on an even more basic level, with so many angels surrounding us, is it possible to have any privacy at all?

And the answer is yes, we can. Angels are not voyeurs. They're not spiritual eavesdroppers. They have a mission to accomplish—our ultimate salvation—and that's what they spend their time focusing on. They aren't too terribly concerned with human gossip or with the thousands of random thoughts that go in and out of our heads every day. They have better things to do.

And, in fact, angels can't read our minds—they don't have that power. Although some theologians have speculated that they might have access to certain regions of our memory and imagination, angels don't know everything that we're thinking from one moment to the next. They're not able to see the hidden workings of our mind. They can't penetrate into the inner sanctum of our conscience, our intellect, and our will. Only God can do that.

This is a crucial point. *We* control the door to our own minds. We open it and close it when we want, insofar as other creatures are concerned. And no matter how wondrous their powers may be, angels are still creatures. Thus, if we want our guardian angels to know what we're thinking, we have to consciously *will* that they know—or we have to purposely talk to them, either out loud or in our mind. That's the equivalent of "opening the door." On the other hand, if we want to keep our thoughts to ourselves, we don't have to do anything. The door to our mind, as a rule, is shut, and impregnable—except, as we just mentioned, to God, who has the power to go through bolted doors. The bottom line is that we can always be alone with God if we want. No angel, no human, and no demon, can ever interfere with that sovereign right given to us by God.

Now, all of that said, we have to remember that angels don't necessarily need the ability to read our minds in order to know what's going on inside our heads. While it's true that they're only "observers," it's also true that they've been observing us since we were conceived in our mothers' wombs! They've been watching us closely all these years, learning about us and the way we do things, listening to our conversations, seeing firsthand our strengths and weaknesses. They know us better than our closest relatives and family members know us—and maybe even better than we know ourselves. And since they're not limited in any way by physical bodies, their ability to learn is not limited either. Angels don't get tired of watching us, they don't have to be "relieved" by other angels in order to sleep, they don't miss anything, they don't forget anything, and they don't misinterpret anything because of human bias.

By our standards, angels are absolute geniuses. The most unenlightened angel is able to understand the interplay of human desires and emotions better than the most brilliant psychologist. Moreover, we can't forget that God is always free to tell them anything he wants about our inner thoughts, temptations, and secrets if he thinks that information might assist them in carrying out their job. The bottom line is that we should never assume that angels are ignorant of anything.

Which brings us to a final point about these mysterious creatures. Up till now we've been talking about angels in terms of their relationship to us. We've defined their powers and abilities only by describing how they affect the lives of human beings on this planet. The problem with this way of thinking is that it's much too self-centered. Angels weren't created *just* for us. That's a gross distortion of the truth. Yes, angels have been charged with the mission of assisting and protecting human beings, but they also have their own lives to consider.

It's easy to forget that angels are just as special and unique as human beings. We tend to lump them all together in one group—as if each of them acted the same way, thought the same way, and went to the same angel store to buy their standard-issue flowing white robes! This couldn't be further from the truth. Thomas Aquinas believed that angels were so different from one another that each one could be considered his own separate species. In other words, each angel has such a unique "personality," and such unique talents and abilities and powers, that no single angel even remotely resembles any other angel. Essentially, the difference between individual angels is as great as the difference between birds and fish; dogs and cats; men and whales. What that means is that the guardian angel given to you by God is more special than you could ever imagine.

We also have to remember that angels have their own happiness, too—a happiness that is completely separate and distinct from ours. In fact, angels don't need human beings at all. They have their own busy angelic lives, with their own interests, their own joys, their own unique past, present, and future, and their own way of loving and serving God. As we mentioned before, the Bible seems to indicate that there are millions and even billions of them, and that they live in some kind of society, with a clear delineation of roles and organized in a hierarchal fashion. Scripture even goes so far as to identify nine specific angelic "orders": Seraphim, Cherubim, Thrones, Dominations, Virtues, Powers, Principalities, Archangels, and Angels. Naturally, it's difficult for us to speculate about the details of this celestial society, but isn't it reasonable to assume that it's at least as fascinating as the societies human beings have built for themselves?

Finally, angels have their own intellect and will. That means they have the ability to think for themselves and choose for themselves. They're not divine robots. Like human beings, they're not programmed. Of course, their intellect works much differently than ours because they don't have bodies and brains and neurological systems through which they have to filter ideas. But their will functions in basically the same manner as ours. When angels were created they had the power to choose between right and wrong, to serve God or work against him, to obey him or disobey him—just as we do today.

And this is really where the story of the angels gets interesting—and frightening. For angels are much more powerful than we are. They have the ability to destroy whole cities, to bring down pestilence and fire upon the earth, and to wreak much more havoc through their evil choices than human beings ever could. That's why it's very eerie to read in the Bible that soon after the creation of the angels, a mighty struggle erupted between them.

What seems to have happened is that one of the angels made a remarkable and surprising decision. God had given all the angels the power to exercise their will freely, and that's exactly what this particular angel did. Only he didn't choose to thank God for creating him, or to praise him or worship him or obey him, as the other angels did. On the contrary, this angel made a clear and irrevocable decision to *reject* God. In fact, not only did he reject God, but he rejected God's entire kingdom as well as God's plan for mankind. Indeed, he rejected mankind itself, with a hatred and intensity so great that Scripture actually speaks of a "war breaking out" in Heaven.

This angel—one of the most supremely gifted and powerful of all the angels in creation—proceeded to launch an all-out rebellion against God. He even succeeded in persuading whole legions of other angels to join with him in his terrible cause.

Who was this brilliant and evil being? What was the nature of his rebellion? What reasons did he have for turning against his Creator? Who were his cohorts, and what, exactly, are they doing today? All of this is the subject of the next chapter.

CHAPTER 4

INVISIBLE EVIL

The Devil and His Demons

Even though the fall of the angels took place at the beginning of time, to read an account of it we have to go to the
last book of the Bible. Scripture is fascinating that way. Every
part of it is infused with meaning from every other part. Despite the fact that the Bible was written over the course of many
centuries by many different authors and in many different
styles and literary forms, we must never forget that the primary
author is God himself, so the whole of it has a profound and
marvelous unity.

Thus, we read in the book of Revelation that

> *There was war in heaven. Michael and his angels fought against*
> *the dragon, and the dragon and his angels fought back. But he*
> *was not strong enough, and they lost their place in heaven. The*
> *great dragon was hurled down—that ancient serpent called*
> *the devil, or Satan, who deceives the whole world. He was hurled*
> *to the earth, and his angels with him. (Rev. 12:7–9)*

Throughout Scripture we see references to this mysterious
"war" that broke out between the "good" angels and the "bad."

We're given glimpses of why the cataclysmic event took place and what happened to the rebel angels as a result.

From the letter of Jude:

> *And the angels who did not keep their positions of authority but*
> *abandoned their own home—these he has kept in darkness,*
> *bound with everlasting chains for judgment on the great Day.*
> *(Jude 1:6)*

From the book of Isaiah:

> *How you have fallen from heaven,*
> *O Lucifer, son of the dawn!*
> *You have been cast down to the earth,*
> *you who once laid low the nations!*
> *You said in your heart,*
> *"I will ascend to heaven;*
> *I will raise my throne above the stars of God;*
> *I will sit enthroned on the mount of assembly,*
> *on the utmost heights of the sacred mountain.*
> *I will ascend above the tops of the clouds;*
> *I will make myself like the Most High."*
> *But you are brought down to the grave,*
> *to the depths of the pit. (Isa. 14:12–15)*

From the book of Ezekiel:

> *You were the model of perfection, full of wisdom and perfect in beauty. You were in Eden, the garden of God; every precious stone adorned you. . . . You were anointed as a guardian cherub, for so I ordained you. You were on the holy mount of God. . . . You were blameless in your ways from the day you were created till wickedness was found in you. (Ezek. 28:12–15)*

Finally, from the lips of Christ:

> *I saw Satan falling like lightning from heaven. (Luke 10:18)*

All of these Scripture verses have to do with the fall of the angels. They do not refer to myth or a legend or a symbol of any kind—as some theologians have erroneously suggested. Rather, they pertain to a real historical event—and a central doctrine of the Christian faith. From these passages, and from the teaching of the early Christian Fathers as well as later theologians, it's possible to piece together the fascinating, frightening, and *true* story of the devil and his demons.

What happened was basically this. God made the angels and gave them free will—just as he gave human beings free will later on. He created the angels to be good. He did not make them evil. But they had a choice. And one of them chose *not* to love and serve God. He chose to reject God. Only he wasn't just *any* angel. He seems to have been very special. This particular angel—who has been called by a variety of names, including Lucifer, Satan, and the devil—seems to have been extremely powerful. He seems to have had a very high "rank" in the hierarchy of angels. Indeed, this angel seems to have been the brightest and most brilliant of all angels. And yet he chose to rebel against God. Why?

According to Scripture, he did so primarily because of pride. "I will raise my throne above the stars of God," he said, "I will make myself like the Most High." At the heart of Satan's rebellion was his desire to assert his independence from God, his desire to be "like God"—not in terms of God's love, but in terms of his power. And this was all due to arrogance and self-love.

Satan then communicated his choice to the other angels. Remember, angels are able to communicate. Yes, they do it differently than we do. They don't speak. They don't express their thoughts in words. But they have an intellect and a will, and through some kind of direct mind-to-mind contact that we don't understand they are able to convey the essence of their thoughts to one another. And this is what Scripture means by a "war" in Heaven. A war is defined as a "state of hostile conflict between nations that usually results in a great loss of life and much suffering." Well, that's exactly what happened. Angels are pure spirits, so any battles they have must primarily be battles of the intellect and will. Their "weapons" are, essentially, arguments. When Satan communicated his rebellious decision to the other angels, he gave them reasons that they should rebel, too. Most of them did not agree with him. Most were grateful to God and loved their Creator. One of these faithful angels has been singled out in Scripture as being particularly close to God—Saint Michael the Archangel. But a good portion of the angels made the same choice as Satan. No one can say for sure how many of these rebel angels there were. But the book of Revelation hints at a number. Speaking of the "great red dragon" that many Christian commentators believe to be the devil himself, Scripture says:

> *And his tail swept away a third of the stars of heaven, and threw them to the earth. And the dragon stood before the woman who was about to give birth, so that when she gave birth he might devour her child. (Rev. 12:4)*

Many theologians believe that the woman in this passage refers to the Virgin Mary, and the child, to Jesus Christ. They also believe that the phrase "a third of the stars" refers to the number of angels who chose to follow Satan. These "bad" angels are known as demons. And since we know that the total number of angels is prodigious, it's reasonable to believe that if a third of them rebelled against God, it's possible that there may be millions or even billions of fallen angels in existence today.

So much for the biblical facts. Now comes the hard part—trying to understand them. And by understanding them, I really mean understanding *him*. The devil. Because I don't think most people do. A recent Harris poll showed that while 60 percent of Americans claim to believe in Satan, a full 40 percent—or *120 million* adults—either disbelieve in him completely or aren't sure of his existence. Moreover, a *Time* magazine poll revealed that of the people who say they *do* believe in the devil, 58 percent think he is "not a living being, but just a symbol of evil."

Beyond this, many people have a cartoonish idea of the Prince of Demons. Some jokingly picture him as a cute little figure with horns and a goatee, carrying a pitchfork and dressed all in red; others think of him in a more serious way as a kind of monster from a horror movie, unspeakably vile and terrifying and nasty-looking. In both cases, the image is one-dimensional. And truth be told, while the devil may be many things, he is not one-dimensional.

Why the widespread disbelief? Why the misconception? The main reason, I think, is that most people are good people, or at least they try to be good, or they want to be good. They don't understand someone who's supposed to be *all* bad *all* the time. Remember, the devil rejected God and rejected Heaven of his own free will. He's someone who *chose* to go to hell. And we all know what hell is supposed to be like. It's a place of ultimate suffering, unlimited torment, unquenchable fire, and eternal darkness; a place of "wailing and gnashing of teeth," a place without one single, solitary inch of sunshine and joy, a place of pain, pain, and more pain. And to make matters even worse, it's forever. If you end up going there, you're stuck there—for good. That's hell.

The frightening thing is that not only is this the popular conception of hell, but it's also a pretty accurate description of the place, theologically speaking. Given this point, and given the fact that we all know how natural it is for living creatures to want to avoid pain and seek pleasure, why in the world would anyone freely decide to go there? Moreover, even if we accepted the fact that Satan and his fellow angels had their own good reasons for wanting to live in hell, why do they seem to have such an obsession with trying to make *us* go there, too? I mean, what's the point? What could they possibly get out of trying to "win souls" and cause our eternal damnation? Why do they spend so much of their time "tempting" us to sin? What do they care about us anyway?

It's quite a mystery. And this is probably why so many people in the secular culture don't pay much attention to the devil, despite the fact that his existence and the existence of the whole demonic realm is an absolute biblical certainty and a major doctrine of the Christian faith. They simply don't "get" him.

How can we make sense of this most famous of all "bad guys"? How can we begin to understand what makes the devil and the demons act the way they do?

As with any criminal, the best thing to do first is to try to come to grips with his motive. Why did the devil reject God, and why did the other angels follow his lead and reject God? The Bible, as we have said, is pretty clear on this point. Satan and his band of rebel conspirators fell from God's grace because of the sin of pride. They were blinded by their own greatness. They overrated their own abilities and powers to such a degree that they disregarded God's supremacy. That's why they refused to take part in God's plan for creation and for his Kingdom. The whole story of the fall of the demons, in fact, can be summed up in the infamous satanic utterance: *Non serviam!* I will not serve.

And that's exactly what the conflict was all about. Neither the devil nor his demon followers wanted to serve God. They didn't want to be his messengers or his angelic "errand boys." They didn't want to go on any missions to assist the human race. They didn't want to do God's bidding, period.

Now, let's try to get to the bottom of this staggering and

unprecedented decision "not to serve," because it's very important, not only for our understanding of what transpired between God and the angels, but also for coming to terms with
what happened later on between God and human beings. Let's
look for a moment at the concept of pride.

Can you remember a time in your life when you were very
mad at someone? Someone who you believed had wronged you?
Had done something he or she had no right to do? Something
that really offended you? Can you remember how you felt at the
time? Can you remember what you said and thought? Try to
recall the specific emotions you were experiencing.

Maybe he or she was a coworker of yours, or a family member, or a neighbor. Maybe this person actually had the nerve to
think that *you* were the one who was at fault, and that you should
be the one to apologize! Do you remember how infuriating that
felt? Perhaps you remember thinking to yourself, "I will never,
ever apologize!"

Now, can you think of a time in your life when you felt this
way, yet *you* were the one who was at fault—*you* were the one
who was wrong all along—and it was only your anger or your
stubbornness or your pride or your stupidity that prevented
you from seeing the truth?

If you're human, chances are something of this kind has
happened to you. We've all been guilty of being wrong and then
compounding our mistake by being foolish and overreacting.
When something like this happens, have you ever noticed how
difficult it can be to admit the truth—especially after you've
worked yourself up so much, or even worse, after you've made
an absolute ass of yourself?

If you're really honest, you might even admit that there have been times during a dispute when it didn't matter if you were right or wrong, times when you were actually content to be angry and resentful and full of animosity—regardless of who was at fault. I'm not speaking here about emotional flare-ups. I'm talking about that point in time after the initial incident has taken place, after the offensive act has been committed, after all the passions have subsided. I'm talking about when the only thing preventing reconciliation is that you just don't think you did anything wrong, or even worse, you don't care—you'd rather stay mad. The truth is that sometimes it feels pretty good to be upset. And sometimes (although let's hope it's not too often) we even prefer that state to seeing the light of reason, and having to go through all the "trouble" of making up and living in peace again.

I'm not saying that it's right to feel this way. It's not. But it's possible to reach a point when it can be more enjoyable to be angry than amiable, more pleasurable to be mean-spirited than merciful. If you've ever experienced anything remotely like this—and most of us have at one time or another—then congratulations! You now know how the devil feels *all the time*!

Let me give you an example from my own past. I remember once when I was about fourteen years old I said some very hurtful things to my mother. I forget the exact circumstances, but I think she had refused to allow my brother and me to go somewhere, and we were both extremely rude to her. In my house, being disrespectful to Mom was simply not tolerated, and when my father got home, my brother and I were immediately sent to our rooms. I remember being angry at my father because, in my mind, my mother had been unfair, and I didn't think the things I had said to her were "bad" enough to justify being punished. Later in the day my younger brother went and sheepishly apologized to my mother. To my surprise, my parents forgave him right away and let him off with a warning. I remember yelling out to my father from my room: "Why is *he* allowed to come out and I can't? That's not fair! I didn't do anything wrong!" My father ignored my pleas and, in fact, yelled back some pretty choice words. I knew from the tone of his voice that he was very upset with me—much more angry than he was at my younger brother, and that this "situation" was far from being over.

But that was fine with me. I was sure I was right, and the fact that my younger brother had gotten off so easy made me even angrier. A few days went by and nothing changed. I was still banished to my room. I went to school, of course, and I could come out of my room for meals, but then I had to go right back in. My father didn't say a word to me or even look at me.

It was getting toward summertime and my room was very small. We didn't have a lot of money, and all seven of us lived in a cramped five-room apartment over a bakery in Brooklyn. But I couldn't have cared less about the uncomfortable heat and humidity. It only made me feel more victimized and consequently more resentful. I certainly didn't give a thought to the fact that I was very lucky to have my own bedroom in the first place. I was the oldest boy, which is an important thing in many Italian homes, and my father wanted me to have that privilege, since I also had a lot more responsibilities than my younger siblings. But I wasn't acting like the "oldest" brother was supposed to act—I was being prideful and stubborn and immature. I had dug in my heels, and absolutely refused to apologize, because I felt that I had been wronged. I remember sitting on my bed in that hot room, with the little fan on, stewing in a pool of my own anger. I couldn't believe my father was making me stay there. I couldn't believe he expected *me* to be sorry. Well, I wasn't going to be the one to give in; if this was to be a war of wills, I was not going to lose—even if I had to stay in that "damn sweat hole" forever.

It was my mother—the one whom I had treated so badly—who finally came to my rescue. She hated seeing me butt heads with my father, and she felt bad that I had to stay in my room. After a few days of this stalemate, she came in to see me and very calmly explained the situation, as only a mother can. She told me that there was no way I was going to win this battle; that my father thought this was a very important lesson I had to learn; that this was no longer about my being disrespectful to her (although that was bad enough), but that in being so prideful I was also showing myself to be ungrateful and unappreciative. My mother told me in no uncertain terms that I had to go to both her and my father and make a real apology—and that I had better do it soon.

After that I felt deflated. I realized that any further stubbornness on my part would be not only fruitless, but silly as well. In my mind this had been a real conflict—a "battle royal." Holding out against my father had made me feel almost equal to him. And I was discovering that this "righteous anger" I was experiencing was actually a very pleasant feeling. But when my mother talked to me, I realized I had been deluding myself.

There was no battle going on—certainly not a battle between equals. I was just being a spoiled brat.

It was tough for me to muster the courage to face up to my father, but I managed to apologize later that day. Knowing I was really wrong made it a little easier. I remember that both my father and my mother accepted my apology right away, but that my father talked to me for a long time about things like pride and stubbornness and respect and humility and the importance of family. He said that the fact that I was older than my brother made what I had done worse, and that I should have known better. I accepted everything he said meekly, and was glad to be done with the argument. Besides, I was tired of staying in my room and wanted to go outside and play with my friends.

The point of the story is that despite the reconciliation that was eventually achieved, there is no doubt that for a short while I really did enjoy being prideful and stubborn, and it didn't matter how uncomfortable I was staying in my room. In fact, the suffering I was experiencing actually made the act of rebellion more pleasurable because it added to my feelings of indignation.

When you think about it, the incident bears a striking resemblance to the story of the fall of Satan! The prideful way I felt at the time and my resolution to willingly put up with discomfort and punishment rather than subject myself to the "humiliation" of apologizing is so similar to how the Prince of Demons felt, it's a wonder I ever got into the business of writing spiritual books!

The devil doesn't think he was wrong either. If you could sit him down in a chair across from you right now and get him to be honest, he would insist that *he* was the victim, that *he* was the one who had been wronged by God. He would say with one hundred percent certitude that God is the real enemy of freedom; that God had no right to subject him and the other angels to some kind of bogus test of moral character; that God had no right to ask him and the other angels to take part in the building up of his sham kingdom—a kingdom where human beings, who are infinitely inferior to angels in terms of their natural abilities, would get to "reign" along with God, right on his throne as the book of Revelation prophesies, a kingdom where God himself would stoop so unbelievably low as to *become a human*, in the person of Jesus Christ. If you could sit Satan down in front of you right now, he would tell you that he had objected to all this "nonsense" from the very beginning, and that it wasn't wrong for him to have rejected God and everything associated with him—since God was being so blatantly unfair.

Ultimately, what the devil objected to was God's *will*—God's will for the universe, God's will for the angels, God's will for human beings. Whether the devil thought he had a better plan than God isn't known. All we can say for sure is that the devil wanted his will to prevail over God's.

That's how he felt at the time, and that's how he feels now. The devil has never changed his mind, and he never will. He *can't*. Let's talk about this point for a moment, because people seem to have a hard time understanding it. They don't see why the devil or at least some of the demons haven't just reconsidered and "come over to our side."

Since angels don't have bodies, they don't have neurological systems. They don't have to process their thoughts through synapses and brain cells. We can't relate to this because all human beings do is "process" ideas. All we do is make choices based on how we filter a thousand different variables though the prism of our bodies. It takes time for us to "see" something, then for our brains to recognize what we see, then to compare it to everything else we've ever seen, to analyze it, measure it, weigh it, and, finally, to make a decision about it. Even the simplest act of "recognizing" a friend or family member is a process. We're able to do it very quickly, of course, but it's not instantaneous. Our brain still has to go through steps.

The point is that whenever there's a physical process involved, there's a possibility of error. There's a chance that we might get our facts wrong, or that we might not get all the information we need, or that we might get the information at the wrong time. There's a chance that we might be too tired to process everything correctly, or that our emotions or our lack of intelligence or our environment or our natural biases might, in some way, cause us to make the wrong decision. There are a million different reasons that it's possible for us to make a mistake, and that's why we're constantly changing our minds. That's why we're always going back and forth, and round and round the same psychological loops, without ever coming to a decision we're really convinced of.

It's not like that for the angels. They don't have to process their thoughts as we do. They "see" whatever they're looking at from every angle, all at once. They don't have to wait around for more information. They don't have to try to "figure out" a problem. They don't have to "sleep on it." Nor do they worry that they made a mistake—because there's never any deliberation involved. They're already in full possession of the facts immediately. All they really have to do is *choose*. And once they make a choice, it's forever, because they've made their choice with complete conviction.

I know it seems like I'm beating this point to death, but once you get it, you won't ever have trouble making sense out of angelic or demonic decisions. The concept actually isn't as alien as it might at first seem. You've made choices like this, too, although you may not realize it because they don't even seem like choices. Just think of something you're completely sure of. Something you're so certain of that you'd "bet your life" on it. It doesn't have to be something big. It can be something very small. Right now, for instance, I'm looking at a red phone that's sitting on my desk. I'm absolutely positive it's red. Why? Because I have all the facts at my fingertips, because my eyes have been checked and I have perfect vision, because I'm not color blind, and simply because I know what the color red is! I've made my decision and it can't be altered. Even if an Angel of the Lord came down from Heaven right now and told me that it was really a blue phone, I would have to respectfully disagree with him and advise him to have his eyes checked at the optometrist office in Heaven! Or I would think he was lying to me, outright, and was therefore a demon. Those are the only two possibilities there are. The only thing outside the realm of possibility would be for me to believe I was wrong about the color of the phone.

Once again, the reason I can feel so strongly about this is because I'm in full possession of all the facts, and I'm in full possession of all my faculties. I don't need any more information, and I don't have to do any more analysis.

Well, that's exactly the way it was for Satan and the rebel

angels when they chose to reject God. Because they were pure spirits, they didn't need to weigh all the variables. They didn't need to do any research on what life would be like without God. They didn't need to "explore all their options." They saw everything at once; they saw all the consequences of their choice at once—and they simply didn't care. They were as certain about their decision to reject God as I am about the color of my phone. And they can no more change that decision than I can change mine about this phone.

In fact, they have even more certainty than I do, because there's always a chance that I might be delusional. Angels and demons, with their amazingly superior intellects, can never be delusional—especially when it comes to the subject of God. And this is what made their fall even more terrible. Because of their spiritual perfection and their powers of insight, they were able to know God in a much more direct way than we can; they were able to see much more clearly into the depths of his greatness than we can. Their knowledge about him from the very beginning, completely unhampered by the limits of physical senses, was incomparably richer than ours. And yet they still rejected him.

When my father explained to me that I was more wrong than my little brother for being nasty to my mother and refusing to apologize, this is what he was trying to get at. I was older, I was smarter, I understood things better—I knew why it was wrong to be disrespectful to my parents. Therefore my actions carried more weight—and they had more serious consequences.

Well, the devil understood the situation perfectly; he knew God better than any creature could know him; he knew he owed God his very existence. Yet he still made a conscious, purposeful, and free choice to reject God. His decision was therefore one of pure spiritual pride, undiluted and unmitigated, and not influenced in any way by the environment, or circumstances, or physical imperfections, or biases, or passions, or his lacking complete information. And because the choice was made by a pure spirit and with complete certainty, it was irrevocable.

Now it's important to understand the wider context of what this rebellion of Satan really meant. In rejecting God, the devil rejected everything God is, everything that God stands for, and everything that resembles God in any way. In rejecting God, the devil rejected truth—because God is Truth—and in so doing, the devil became a "liar and the father of all lies." In rejecting God, the devil rejected goodness—because God is Goodness—and in so doing, he embraced all that is evil and hurtful and painful in the world. In rejecting God, the devil rejected light—because God is Light—and in so doing, he sank into the abyss of eternal darkness and gloom known as hell.

This may sound poetic, but it's true. The decision to reject God was completely life-altering, and once it was made, it was fixed forever. Does the devil care that he now lives in the midst of darkness, suffering, deceit, and evil? Not really. No more than I cared about being in my hot, humid, oppressive little room when I was being punished. Indeed, the devil would rather be where he is than anywhere else in all creation. Not that he's "happy" or "joyful" in any way—he's not; he's experiencing real pain. But in a certain sense he does "like" being where he is, just as he "likes" the fact that he's suffering. It only adds to his resentment of God. It only adds to his indignation at being victimized.

It only adds fuel to his hatred. It only makes him want to offend God more.

And that's his simple object: to offend God. Indeed, that's the object of all the demons. After all, what do you do when you hate someone? I mean really *hate* someone? What do you do when you feel someone is responsible for all your troubles, for all your unhappiness? At the very least, your inclination is going to be to want to hurt that person, to cause that person pain.

But let me ask you a question. What if you can't do that? What if it's impossible? What if the person you hate is all-powerful and can't suffer? What if the person you hate is God and can't be hurt in any conventional way?

The only option you have is to do the next best thing. If you can't hurt God himself, you hurt that which bears the image of God. You hurt that which resembles God most, that which was made in God's likeness. In other words, you do everything you can to hurt those miserable, fallen, and inferior creatures known as *human beings*.

And that's exactly what the devil and his demons have tried to do throughout history. They've done everything in their power to lie, trick, tempt, foil, injure, humiliate, mock, and kill human beings. By attempting to undermine God's plan for the salvation of mankind, they've been able to effectively lash out at God. They've been able to mock him and offend him. And the knowledge that they can be successful in bringing us down has given them an evil pleasure, a satisfaction of their demonic pride.

The scary thing about all this is that it's true. It's not a horror movie, it's not make-believe, it's not mythology, it's not superstition. It's the Christian faith. Human beings are the principal target of the devil and his demons. We're the "big game" that's being hunted. If the demons can persuade us to turn against God, that represents the only "victory" they can ever achieve against the One whom they despise so much.

Ultimately, this is what constitutes the great battle for souls—the great battle between good and evil that has plagued humanity since time immemorial. And it has tremendous importance for each and every one of us. Because when we come to the end of our lives, and our bodies are separated from our souls, our acceptance or rejection of God will become fixed forever—just as the decision of the angels and the demons was fixed forever.

Let me repeat that. With death, all deliberation comes to an abrupt end. The decision we've freely made as of that time won't be able to be changed. Remember, what makes our choices different from those of the angels and demons is that we have mechanized bodies. All the decisions we make are filtered and processed—and that takes time. So we have the ability to change our minds, to reconsider, to correct our mistakes, to repent of our sins, to accept or reject God's will. But we're not always going to have this advantage—because we're not always going to have these bodies. Someday after we die but before we experience the Ressurection, we're just going to be spirits. We're going to be like the angels. And therefore the state we're in at the moment of death is what will determine our *final* choice about God.

The object of the devil and his demons is to influence that decision. They can't make the decision for us, because we have free will, but they can try to *persuade* us. They can attempt to make us come to the same conclusion they did—namely, that God has no right to ask us to obey his commands, that he has no right to ask us to follow his will, that he has no right to ask us to live life on his terms.

How they go about persuading us is fascinating. Since demons are fallen angels, they have great intellectual as well as supernatural powers, including the ability to manipulate human beings, psychologically, and the ability to propagate widespread falsehoods. In cases of possession, demons have been shown to have the power to do all sorts of frightening things: to move material objects, to levitate, to employ curses and witchcraft and sorcery; to manipulate the basic elements of nature, to infest houses and other physical things; and even to control animals. Like angels, demons have their own individual "personalities." Some are more mocking, some are more proud, some are more hateful, and some are more envious. Each of them has his own way of "tempting," his own particular area of diabolical specialty. The demonic network of communication, the demonic hierarchy, indeed the whole demonic world is every bit as real and actual as ours.

But we're getting ahead of ourselves. In this chapter we've tried to shed some light on why the devil and his demons would want to be the way they are. What they actually do to tempt human beings and what God does to counter that temptation through the power of his grace and his Church is something that we'll examine more carefully in a little while.

Before we delve into that, though, we first need to spend some time discussing the "target" of all this demonic activity. We need to talk about this creature that God has created "in his image and likeness," a creature part spiritual, part physical; part human, but with a capacity for the divine. We need to talk about this strange animal that lives and grows and deteriorates and dies, but at the same time has within it something everlasting and immortal; something infinitely brighter than the brightest star; something destined one day to be reunited to its body and experience the glorious power of resurrection. In other words, we need to talk about what is invisible in *us*—we need to talk about that mysterious thing known as the *human soul*.

THE INVISIBLE SOUL

I remember the first time I ever saw a dead body. I must have been seven or eight years old. My aunt had passed away after a long battle with cancer. She was only in her early fifties, and I was sad because she lived right around the corner from my family and always treated me nicely and sometimes even gave me little presents that made me feel special. She was just a simple person, sweet and warm and good, and I remember feeling very bad when she died.

My father didn't want me and my brothers and sister to go to the funeral because we were so young. But there was no one to watch us, so we all went to the funeral home and stayed in the waiting area outside the main room, where the wake was being held. At some point, though, I got bored and decided to sneak into the room. I remember walking along the side of the wall, past the flowers and the people crying, right up to the coffin, where I stood for a few seconds staring at my dead aunt's face. It was an eerie experience. I distinctly remember being frightened.

But I also remember something else. I remember thinking to myself that it was very odd that I should feel scared. After all, this was my aunt—my aunt whom I loved. Just a few weeks earlier, looking at her would have made me smile; in fact, I would have run right up to her and hugged her and given her a big kiss. Now the mere sight of her was enough to make me recoil in horror. How could that be? How could that peaceful face in the coffin inspire such fear and revulsion? I had seen her sleeping before, and she didn't look so much different now. Yet I knew there *was* a difference. I knew that even though it looked like her, it wasn't *her* anymore. I knew that whatever it was that had made her my aunt was no longer there. And it was this knowledge that made her lifeless body so terrifying.

The point of this story is that even when you're a child and completely ignorant of theology, it's possible to understand— through intuition—that the human soul exists. It's even possible to recognize—at least on some level—that the primary purpose of the soul is to give life to the body; and that when the soul departs the body dies.

Yet the soul is much more than just the "animating principle" of the body. Yes, it gives us life, but it also makes human beings human. It's what separates us from the rest of creation. Remember the famous quote from Hamlet?

> *What [a] piece of work is a man, how noble in reason, how infinite in faculties, in form and moving how express and admirable, in action how like an angel, in apprehension how like a god! the beauty of the world; the paragon of animals. . . .*
> (Hamlet 2.2. 303–7)

Shakespeare was right. Man *is* an incredible creation. As we said earlier, to be human is to be an amazing kind of hybrid: part spirit, part matter. The part of us that is material is easy to recognize—just look in the mirror. The part that's spiritual—our soul—can't be seen, because its nature is to be invisible. But nevertheless, it's just as real, just as true, and just as alive as our physical bodies.

And, of course, just because our spirits can't be seen with the human eye doesn't mean that they can't be seen and known by the mind. They most certainly can. This is a point that atheists always seem to miss. Human beings are constantly doing things that demonstrate that we're much more than material bodies. Show me any living creature, for instance, that will go against its own instinct, its own nature, its own physical desire to avoid pain and, instead, willingly suffer hardships and even sacrifice its life—as humans so often do—for love, honor, abstract principles, and other invisible realities. It just isn't done. Humans are able to recognize higher spiritual realities and take actions that directly contradict their physical well-being only because there's a part of us that *is* spiritual and understands that the spirit is just as important as the body, and that it must be nurtured—even sometimes at the expense of the body, even sometimes at the expense of physical life itself.

In other words, if we were just physical bodies, we would be able to do only those things that physical bodies can do. But that's not the case. It's obvious that we can do plenty of things that go beyond the realm of the physical. As we said in the first chapter of this book, those who deny the existence of the soul would have us believe that the whole world of the mind, the whole inner world of ideas, everything we can conceive of having to do with beauty, art, music, poetry, truth, creation, redemption, Heaven, hell, love, kindness, sacrifice, and evil—all of the great desires of the human heart that have caused the rise and fall of countless civilizations—all of it is simply the result of the random movement of atoms and molecules!

When you think about it, it's really preposterous. There was an underrated movie from several years ago called *Shallow Hal* that underscores this point. The premise of the film is that a young man named Hal, who only cares about shallow, selfish things, suddenly gets the power to see other human beings the way they are on the *inside*, in their spirit. When he meets an extremely heavyset girl, for instance, he doesn't recognize the fact that she's overweight. All he sees is her beauty. That's because on the inside she truly is beautiful. In fact, she's one of the kindest, most caring human beings he has ever met. Thus, while everyone else around him, including the girl's family and friends, see her as a fat, unattractive woman—someone, in fact, to be ashamed of—Hal sees an absolutely gorgeous blonde and he quickly falls in love with her.

The movie is a comedy, so it has a lot of slapstick humor and fat jokes. But the underlying point is really very profound. There's one scene in particular that is quite touching. The overweight girl whom Hal is in love with happens to do volunteer work at the pediatric burn unit of the local hospital. The children in the ward are extremely disfigured; some have even lost half their faces. When Hal first meets them, he can't see any of that. He can't see that they're maimed and scarred and "ugly." Instead, he sees what's invisible to everyone else—what's underneath the exterior, physical reality. And what's underneath is wonderful. To him, they appear to be normal little kids, with bright, shining, innocent faces. In fact, he can't understand why they're in the hospital in the first place. He spends the whole day playing games with them, telling them how cute they are, making them laugh, and kissing them all over their faces. The nurses and doctors and other volunteers are amazed. They can't understand why Hal doesn't seem the slightest bit repulsed by the children's physical appearance.

Later on, when Hal no longer has this special ability to see the invisible inside of people, he goes back to the hospital to look for his girlfriend. It's only then that he sees for the first time what the children in the burn ward really look like. And, of course, he's shocked. In fact, he doesn't even recognize them. Deprived of his special power, he's able to see only what the world sees—little creatures that resemble lepers, grotesque and deformed. They recognize him, however, and are overjoyed that he has returned. But they can't understand the change in him; why he has suddenly become so hesitant and nervous around them. Once he catches on, though, he manages to pull himself together and act the same affectionate way he did earlier. But it's a struggle for him, and he's deeply disturbed.

We all know that human beings are a lot more than what they appear to be. We all know that what's on the outside represents only the tip of the iceberg and is often very misleading. We know that there's something inside us that makes us who we really are. In other words, without any knowledge of the Bible or religion, we know that the human soul exists.

Now, of course, I'm simplifying things. This is not meant to be a theology textbook. My objective is to show that there's more to being human than just having a certain kind of DNA. We all know instinctively that there are really two worlds—an outside world and an inside world. And what happens on the inside is every bit as real and true as what happens on the outside. Sometimes more so.

What accounts for what takes place on the inside? Simply this: At the very moment of conception, God infuses into each and every human being an invisible soul; and this soul, created out of nothing, is everlasting. Yes, it has a beginning, but once it has been created, God never allows it to go out of existence. *Never.* And it's this immortal soul that gives life to our bodies and separates us from the rest of material creation.

Now, all kinds of misconceptions and errors have arisen over the centuries concerning the "connection" between body and soul. As we've already noted, there are people who deny the link completely and believe that there's no such thing as a soul. Then there are those who acknowledge that there might be some kind of spiritual substance that gives life to all the animals and plants on the earth—but they stop there. They don't make any distinction between these kinds of spirits and the human soul. On the other end of the spectrum are those who view the body as something corrupt and evil. To them, humans are primarily spiritual creatures that happen to *have* physical bodies, and they believe that the only way we can ever achieve true peace and happiness is if we divorce ourselves from what they consider to be our bodily "prisons."

All of these beliefs miss the mark. The Christian approach is by far the most balanced—and the one that rings truest. It teaches that human beings are *both* body and spirit, with neither one having absolute primacy over the other. At the moment of conception these distinct entities are fused together in a way we can't completely comprehend. And while it's true that the soul and body separate from each other when we die, that separation is meant to be only temporary. One day, after what is commonly known as the Resurrection, the body and soul will be reunited again in Heaven. The reason that the soul and body are destined to be together is that God created them to be one composite entity. We're not like the angels, who are pure spirits, and we're not like the rocks, which are pure matter. We're both—united together, perfectly. And while other animals may possess souls that animate their bodies, we're the only ones whose souls are, by nature, immortal, and more important, are made in the image and likeness of God.

We hear that phrase a lot—the "image and likeness of God." It's important to understand it because it's really the key to unlocking many of the mysteries involving the soul. What it basically means is that, like God, humans have the ability to think on a higher plane. They have the ability to appreciate truth and beauty, and the ability to grasp the moral law and to make free choices based upon that understanding. Moreover, it means that humans have the ability to "create" in a manner similar to the way God creates.

G. K. Chesterton, in that difficult but wonderful book *The Everlasting Man*, speaks about the paintings done by the earliest human beings on the walls of some caves in southwestern France. When these Paleolithic paintings were discovered, they caused quite a stir in the scientific community. They were very simply done and consisted mainly of animals and human figures and handprints. Yet despite the lack of substantive detail, all kinds of wild pronouncements were made about the life of these "cavemen" who—scientists said—must necessarily have been very brutal, primitive, and animal-like creatures who did nothing but hunt in tribes and gather food and make war. All of these "facts" and more—including theories about the strange religious taboos of the first human beings—were deduced from a few random paintings on the walls of some caves. Yet none of the scientists made the most obvious deduction—the only one that really makes sense—namely, that from the earliest recorded moment of his existence on this planet, the creature known as Man was an *artist*.

Art is the signature of the man, Chesterton said. It's a testimony to something absolute and unique that belongs to human beings, and human beings alone. And this "unique something" that separates us from the other animals isn't a matter of degree; it's a matter of kind. A monkey doesn't draw clumsily and man cleverly. A monkey doesn't draw at all. He doesn't even begin to draw. It doesn't matter how brilliant or special a monkey he is. He can't draw because the practice of art belongs to a realm entirely alien to monkeys—the realm of creativity. And it's only because human beings possess invisible souls, made in the image and likeness of God—the Creator of everything— that they, too, can be creators.

If you happen to be the kind of person who leans toward atheism or materialism, you might want to take a little time to ponder the world of the arts. Just visit a museum, or better yet, go to a concert or listen to the radio. Find a piece of music that really moves you—one that makes you feel positively joyful and causes a tingle to run up your spine. Then ask yourself this question: Could this have been produced by a biological organism? More specifically, could it have been produced by a mere ball of flesh containing a little water, a few chemicals, with an electric current running through it? Because that is basically how doctors describe the human brain. Could this music that makes my whole being soar above the clouds and transcend this corrupt, decaying world around me really be the creation of some *thing* that is doomed to decay?

It's pretty hard to believe. That's why the existence of music, paintings, literature, movies, cities, and civilizations proves better than any logical argument the existence of the soul. And, in fact, when you think about it, our creative powers extend far beyond ordinary cultural achievements. For *all* human beings are creators, regardless of whether or not they have any talent, regardless of whether or not they practice the arts. The reason is that all of us have the ability to "create" ourselves. We have the ability to make ourselves into the kind of people we want to be.

And this is really the whole basis for the personal development industry—an industry that is founded on the belief that human beings are the masters of their fate and the authors of their destiny. The reason that such a belief can be held with confidence is that it's basically true. All of us have the spiritual power—given to us by God—to interpret the events of our lives in any way we choose. We may not be able to control the outside world, but we have absolute control over the inside world. We control our mind and how we perceive reality. We control the beliefs we have that shape how we respond to people, places, and things. We decide whether or not something that happens to us is either a "problem" or a "challenge," an "obstacle" or an "opportunity." It's because of our ability to represent exterior facts to ourselves in ways that are empowering that it's possible to take anything that happens in life—even the most terrible suffering—and transform it into something that benefits us in the long run. Thus we always have the ability to make ourselves into the kind of people we want to be.

This power to create ourselves is something that anyone can make use of, regardless of IQ, financial background, or level of education. If this weren't the case, there wouldn't be so many self-made millionaires in the world; there wouldn't be so many people who have overcome great suffering and hardships and turned their lives completely around. All you have to do is read a few self-help books and you'll see dozens of examples of people who have gone through all kinds of abuse and violence and grief yet still have managed to pull some kind of good out of their tragedy.

All the folks who have been able to reshape their lives in this remarkable manner have one thing in common. They've all found a way to reach down into the depths of their being and tap into something greater than their physical bodies, something more meaningful than the dance of electrons and protons in their brains, something infinite and never-ending. In a word, they've all managed to harness the power of their invisible souls.

I read an interesting story recently about the creative power of the human spirit. There was a young man who had two small daughters. The man was very hardworking and dedicated to his job, but he loved his children more than anything and made sure that he spent a lot of quality time with them. He would take them to a little amusement park near their home on the weekends. In this park there happened to be a merry-go-round that the girls liked to go on, and the man got into the habit of putting them on the ride and then sitting down on a little red bench nearby to watch them. He did this every weekend, and sometimes he would find himself getting bored when they were busy having fun on the rides and he was left to himself.

One day when he was sitting in his usual spot on the red bench in front of the merry-go-round, daydreaming and tapping his fingers on his leg, a thought came into his head. It was just a simple thought. Not a great thought. Not a revolutionary thought. Not even a particularly original thought. It was just an average thought that anyone might have had if they had been sitting on the same bench, week after week, bored because they had nothing to do. The thought was this: "Somebody should make an amusement park where the adults could have some fun, too."

That was it. That was the whole substance of the thought that came into the man's head. In fact, the only thing that makes this story remotely interesting is that the name of the man into whose head the thought popped was none other than Walt Disney! And the idea he had that day became the genesis for Disneyland.

Now, Walt Disney was not some kind of super genius. He did not have the intellect of Einstein or Aristotle. Nor did he have the talent of da Vinci or Michelangelo. Nor did he have the looks and physique of a Hollywood movie star. Yet he was able to create something that has given more real joy to people (especially children) than many of the loftiest achievements of the world's greatest geniuses. How was he able to do that?

There's only one explanation. Walt Disney managed to tap into that part of himself that was more than material. He managed to tap into that part of himself that was made in the image and likeness of God, who is the source of all creativity. Bear in mind that I'm not making any moral statements here about Disney or anyone else who has accomplished great things. I'm only saying that the human soul—designed by God to reflect his own awesome powers—is capable of performing all sorts of wonders, with or without the aid of natural abilities.

The important thing to understand about all this is that the main purpose of the soul is to enable us to be elevated—through the power of God's grace—to a totally new level; a new level of knowledge, a new level of understanding, a new level of love, and a new level of creative ability. It's a critical point to get because unless you fully appreciate the value of the soul, it's going to be impossible to make any sense of the devil's desire to destroy us.

You see, up until now we've been talking about the soul only in terms of the marvelous *earthly* things it can help us to accomplish. But there's much more to it than this. There's a whole mysterious, metaphysical component having to do with *divine life* that we need to discuss. And it's this area that the devil is primarily interested in.

Basically, it all comes down to the relationship we're privileged to share with God. We said at the start of this book that God created us freely. He didn't have to make us. He didn't have to make anything. He was completely happy on his own. God is a family within himself—Father, Son, and Holy Spirit. He didn't create us because he was lonely or needed company. Nor was he depressed or bored. God created the universe and everything in it for one reason and one reason only—because he wanted to *share* the life and happiness that he already had from all eternity.

And so he created the angels, the stars, the mountains, the oceans, the animals, and the plants—all of his own free will. He shared his life on many different levels, and because of this all of creation reflects the life of God to some degree. Just as an artist puts something of himself into everything he makes, so God has left his stamp on every work of his creation. In fact, whenever we enjoy something beautiful in the world—whether it's a sunset, a song, or a puppy—the real reason that we're experiencing that pleasure is that we're responding to the "echo" of God in that creation.

Now, what makes us so special is that of all the material creatures in the world, we are the only ones who are able to communicate with our Creator. We're the only ones who are able to have a knowing, deliberate, free, profound, two-way *relationship* with him. The rocks can't do that. The rivers can't do that. The monkeys can't do that. We're the only ones who can consciously say: "We are creatures. We have a Creator."

And yet the amazing thing is, we don't usually say that. In fact, we don't usually call God our Creator at all. What we actually say in practice is that we are *sons and daughters*. And we commonly refer to God as our *Father*. And this is where the discussion of our invisible soul gets really interesting. Because the question that naturally arises is: How in the world can we speak to God on such familiar terms? Think about it. God is the almighty, all-knowing, infinite Creator of the universe—the maker of the sun, the moon, and the stars. There's such a ridiculously huge gulf

separating him and us. How can we even think of being so intimate with him? How can we presume that God even wants that
kind of relationship with us? In a word, how can we dare to be
so bold?

The answer, once again, is bound up in the mystery of Christmas. For the only excuse we have for being so bold and pre-
sumptuous is that God took the form of a human in the person
of Jesus Christ. And it is in Christ—who is the "Son" in the
phrase "Father, Son, and Holy Spirit"—that we can begin to
share in the relationship of child to father.

Yes, we're all God's children, but those of us fortunate
enough to be Christians actually get to share in Christ's Son-
ship with the Father in a uniquely special way—if we choose.

What makes this possible is the power of the human soul.
When God became one of us, he essentially took on our human
nature so that we could have some of his divine nature. He *elevated* humanity to an unimaginable degree. The great signifi-
cance of being baptized into the Christian faith is that the
baptized person's soul is mysteriously initiated into the very life
of Christ. And since Christ is the Son of God, a Christian actually possesses a new kind of life—the life of a son or daughter in
God's family.

Why is that so important? Well, how would you like it if you
could somehow become an heir to say, Donald Trump or Bill
Gates—or better yet, some fabulously wealthy king? Wouldn't
that be something that would change your life? Wouldn't it give
you resources that you could use to help yourself and others in
ways that you never dreamed possible? Well, that's basically

what being a Christian means. It means that you are part of the family of the King of Heaven—and heir to the fortune of the King.

Remember, it was Christ, the Son of God, who began his public ministry with the words: "Behold, the Kingdom of God is upon you!" And it was Christ who inaugurated this new Kingdom—a kingdom very different from any that has ever existed before. For it isn't an earthly paradise or a political utopia of any kind, but rather it is a spiritually based *way of living* in which all the sons and daughters of God can live together acknowledging God's total sovereignty over their lives and sharing in his divine nature.

And that is precisely what living in the Kingdom of God means. It means living on a higher spiritual plane of life—one animated by heroic, selfless love—the kind of love that God practices. It means being truthful, because God is Truth. It means being just, because God is Justice. It means being loving, because God is Love. It means respecting life, because God is Life. It means living your life on a much higher level than is humanly possible.

If you're able to do this—to actually live "in the Kingdom" on a regular basis—then you know what will happen? Not only will you be happy, but the very deepest longings of your heart will be satisfied. We talked a little before about music. We said the reason that it can move us so deeply is because it has the power to speak to us about an *aspect* of God and his Kingdom. Just an aspect. Well, imagine how it feels to actually be part of the Kingdom *all the time*. Ask anyone who is truly holy, and they will give you the answer: it feels pretty spectacular!

None of this is to say that by living your life this way you will be immune from suffering. You won't be. As long as you're on this planet, you're going to have your share of problems. What it does mean is that there won't be any problem in your life bigger than your spirit; there won't be any problem that will have the power to permanently disrupt the profound sense of joy and peace that you feel on a consistent basis—a peace that, in the words of Scripture, "transcends all understanding."

Ultimately, this is why Christians are supposed to be joyful people. It's why they're supposed to follow the commandments and the law of love without grumbling and complaining. It's why they're supposed to reject sin. Not because of any fear of punishment. Not because they're being "forced" to carry some enormous burden or follow some rigid list of dos and don'ts. It's because their hearts have been captured by the Kingdom. It's because they're actually *in love* with the King. That's what being a Christian really means. And when you have that mindset, all the so-called rules and regulations make perfect sense. In fact, the burden of having to follow them actually feels pretty light compared with the oppressively heavy load that nonbelievers have to shoulder all the time—the burden of loneliness and emptiness and eternal nothingness.

Now, do all Christians live this way? Obviously not! But can they, objectively speaking? Do they have the power to if they wish? The answer is yes, they absolutely do! And, ultimately, that's the purpose of our invisible souls. Besides animating our bodies and reflecting the image of God, the main job of the soul is to elevate us to the degree that we're able to share in the life of the Kingdom of God.

We're *all* meant to be part of this kingdom. We're all meant for glory. Tragically, though, not all of us get to experience it—either here or in the next life. The fact is, hell is a real place. It really exists. And there are people who really go there. C. S. Lewis once said that there is no such thing as an "ordinary human being." Every single person you encounter is destined to be either a king or a queen in Heaven—or a wretched slave in hell.

The fact is that there are many powerful invisible forces that are working against us. And these forces will stop at nothing to achieve their objective: to keep our souls from being in union with God, to keep us from sharing in his divine life, to keep us from experiencing true joy, to keep us from creating ourselves in ways that show the world what our spirits are really like—in a word, to keep us from living in the Kingdom.

That's the next subject we're going to tackle—and it's a very scary subject indeed. For there is a great invisible battle going on—a battle that's going on *right now*. You may not hear the whistle of bullets flying in the air, or the explosions of grenades, or the horrible screams of people wounded by gunfire; you may not see the carnage of bodies and the rubble in the streets; you may not smell the odor of sulfur and fire and rotting flesh. But it's all there. Right outside your window. Just as C. S. Lewis said there was no such thing as an "ordinary" person, so there's no such thing as a truly "peaceful day."

For peace itself—outside of the kind that God bestows—is an illusion. As surely as you are reading these words right now, there is an invisible battle raging all around you—a battle between Heaven and hell, between angels and demons, between darkness and light, between evil and grace; a battle in which there has never been a single truce or so much as one solitary second of silence from the very beginning of time; a battle that is taking place at every moment of the day, every day of your life, in every house in every town in every city in every country of the world.

And it is the invisible battle for souls.

INVISIBLE WARFARE

The Diabolical Battle for Souls

In the movie *The Exorcist*, an older priest sums up the nature of diabolical warfare by warning his younger protégé: *the attack will be psychological.* This perfectly describes the method the devil and his demons use when trying to tempt human beings. Everything is done in the mind. Horror movies notwithstanding, demons don't usually appear to us in all their gory, terrifying reality. They don't normally show themselves to us at all. The reason is that they don't *want* to scare the daylights out of us. That's not their objective. If they appeared to us in that manner, they would be revealing themselves plainly to us—and we would know for sure that they exist. The end result of this "unmasking" would be that our faith in *all* spiritual realities—including God—would most likely increase. And that's the last thing that demons want.

Let me say that again, because it's a critical point. The devil and his demons don't really want us to believe in their existence. From a purely strategic point of view, it's much more effective for them to remain unseen, because that's the tactic that best encourages atheism—something upon which we'll have more to say shortly. It's far better for the demons to hide from us, to stay way in the background, to use every kind of camouflage imaginable in order to keep us from recognizing the active role they are playing in our lives. That's why their attack is always psychological. Because you can't "see" what goes on inside the head. The attack is completely invisible.

What demons therefore specialize in doing is making suggestions to our psyches. They essentially smuggle thoughts into our brain and place images before our mind's eye. Remember, demons are angels—fallen angels, yes, but angels nonetheless. Thus they have the same kind of powers that other angels have. Recall what we said about this subject earlier. Angels are pure spirits who have the ability to communicate directly to us without any kind of language. They're not bound by matter and space, so they can go anywhere they want at any time. They don't get tired, they don't get hungry, they don't get bored. They can enter your home or your place of business and come right up next to you at any hour of the day, whether you're awake or asleep. And it doesn't matter how many locks you have on your doors or what kind of fancy alarm system you've installed in your house. Demons have the power to pass through all barriers completely undetected. And they're perfectly free to stay at your side, unobserved, for days, months, years, and decades, observing every single move that you make.

Moreover, demons are brilliant—they're much smarter than you or I or any human being. God created them to be superintelligent. Because they don't have bodies, they don't have to process their thoughts through neurons and synapses and brain cells. Thus they're able to "think" at speeds infinitely faster than the fastest computer. They also don't forget anything. Because of these abilities they have the power to know you as well as or better than you know yourself. In fact, you can safely assume that if a particular demon has latched on to you, he has probably been observing you closely with his high-powered intelligence for years. And he hasn't missed a thing! He's aware of all your weaknesses, all your failings, all your sins, all your deep, dark secrets. Any skeletons you have in your closet are known to him and can be pulled out and used against you psychologically in a devastatingly effective way at any time.

It's a scary thought, I know, and I wish it weren't true. The most frightening part is that the demon who is at your side right now actually wants you to suffer, die, and experience everlasting torment. That's his greatest desire. And he's going to do everything in his power to make that wish come true. He'll lie, cheat, steal, kill, and do anything else he can get away with in order to accomplish his mission and win your soul for his father in hell.

Of course, some academics like to scoff at the notion that demons really exist. They teach in their university courses that the devil is just a "theological construct," something we merely use to "symbolize" evil. What nonsense! Ask anyone who has really suffered in life—especially anyone who has been at the mercy of a drug or alcohol or sexual addiction—ask them if they believe in the devil; ask them if they have any doubt whatsoever about the existence of a real, personal, evil, spiritual being who has entrapped and enslaved them and tortured them. See if they don't give you an answer that is totally different from what the skeptical academics will tell you.

The Rev. John Corapi likes to tell a story about the time he rode with a police officer through the streets of Los Angeles. There was a call on the radio about a shooting involving a teenage girl. It seems that this girl had run away from home a year earlier, when she was only fourteen. She'd had a very troubled family life, and somehow she had managed to save enough money to go to LA in the hopes of becoming an actress. She was very pretty and sweet and naive.

One of the predators who specialize in spotting troubled young teens saw this girl get off the bus and, of course, offered to "help" her. You can guess what happened next. Within a few weeks he had successfully gotten her addicted to heroin, and then quickly turned her out on the street as a prostitute. When Father Corapi met up with her, she was dead. Apparently the pimp had become angry with her over something, and in a drug-induced rage he had shot her and dumped her body in a garbage bin. That's the way she was when Father Corapi saw her—dirty, bloody, dead, and surrounded by filth and garbage. Naturally he was terribly shaken. He realized that this girl was somebody's daughter, and in talks he subsequently gave on the subject of demonic activity and addictions he would always end with the sobering line: "And don't you forget—that's exactly where the devil wants your son or daughter—*dead in a garbage can!*"

We can't forget that, either. As we delve deeper into the theology of evil, we need to keep in mind that this isn't just an abstract discussion. This is a real battle, with real casualties, being waged by real spiritual beings who really want to destroy us.

At the same time, if we're ever going to resist these powerful forces, we have to separate ourselves a bit from the more frightening aspects of spiritual warfare and attempt to understand exactly what the enemy is trying to do. In other words, we have to try to get a handle on demonic strategy. And there's really only one way to do that. We must go back and review a story that we're all familiar with, but which few of us rarely bother to think about. I'm talking about the strange tale of Adam and Eve in the Garden of Eden. It's there that we see the prototype for the devil's game plan of invisible warfare.

Recall that, according to the book of Genesis, God created the first man and woman and placed them in the middle of Paradise. At the time there was no such thing as suffering or death. Adam and Eve were happy, and God gave them complete freedom to do anything they liked. Except for one thing. He absolutely forbade them to eat from a certain tree in the middle of the garden because, he said, its fruit would kill them. It's important to note that God didn't prohibit Adam and Eve from eating from any of the other trees—just this one. He said that if they ate from this tree, they would die. He was very clear on this point. And this forbidden tree had a very peculiar name. It was called the *tree of the knowledge of good and evil.*

It was at this moment that the devil first made his appearance in human history. In the guise of a serpent he slithered his way into the Garden of Eden and tempted Adam and Eve to do exactly what God had told them not to do—to eat from this special tree. In order to accomplish this, the devil did something very simple. He lied to them. He told them that they would *not* die if they ate this fruit; indeed, he told them that just the opposite would happen—they would become like God.

We all know the end of the story. Adam and Eve chose to listen to the devil, and in doing so they disobeyed God. It was a completely free choice, and they knew what the consequences would be. But they went ahead and did it anyway, out of pride—the very same sin that Satan himself had committed earlier. And it was because of this free decision to sin that evil and suffering and death first entered the world and were passed on to future generations of mankind, right up to the present day.

That's the well-known story of the "fall of man." The profound spiritual truths that it conveys have tremendous importance for us today. What are they? For the sake of brevity, we'll mention just a few. First, God told Adam and Eve that they could eat of any tree in the Garden except one. That's significant. What God was essentially saying was that human beings were not created to be slaves. Human beings were meant to have freedom—a lot of freedom. But there are limits to that freedom. You don't have the right to kill an innocent person, for example. You don't have the right to steal. You don't have the right to commit adultery. Yes, you may have the ability to do these things. You may even be able to do them legally. But you don't have the *right* to do them. Authentic freedom consists in the power to choose between the vast number of things and activities in the world that are good. Freedom doesn't mean that you can do anything you want, anytime you want. That's not freedom at all. That's *license*. And God never gave human beings the right to license—not when he first created us, and not now.

Another great truth contained in this story is that the most terrible kind of evil is *moral* evil. Most of us have trouble believing this. Most of us think that the worst kind of evil is of the physical variety—death, war, destruction, diseases, poverty, and so on. Yet one of the most important lessons of the story of Adam and Eve is that moral evil is far worse in the eyes of God than any of those things. After all, it wasn't a germ or a virus or an earthquake that caused the downfall of our first parents. It was a sin—an invisible decision to disobey God, followed by a disobedient action. That was the reason death and suffering entered the world. And that is the reason, ultimately, why we still have to deal with those unpleasant realities today.

This is going to be a critical point to remember when we discuss the topic of suffering later on. Because although it's true that the devil loves to see us in pain, it's also true that he's not overly concerned with the idea of pain itself. Like God, he's far more interested in the moral dimension of human suffering. In other words, he's more concerned with how our pain affects us on the inside, how it affects our invisible soul. Is it uniting us with God, or is it separating us from him? Is it causing us to move toward the Kingdom of Heaven or away from it? Those are the kinds of questions the devil is always asking.

If you could see what moral evil does to a person *on the inside*, you would understand the devil's motivation. Moral evil is like an acid that eats away a person's soul. It weakens it at first, causing it to deteriorate and crumble, and then it consumes it, little by little, until the only thing remaining is a hollow shell—a hollow shell in which the evil is able to live comfortably and safely. Once the soul has been taken hold of in this fashion, the person has very little freedom left. That's why preachers are always saying that sin "enslaves" a person.

And isn't that true? If you steal, you don't steal once in a while—you're usually a slave to stealing. Likewise, if you envy people, you're usually a slave to envy. If you're gluttonous, you're usually a slave to gluttony. If you're a liar, you're usually a slave to lying. If you're lustful, you're usually a slave to lust. The reason is that these sins have eaten away at the inner core of your soul—like maggots—and built a nice, safe warm home there, from which they're able to exercise control over you. And ultimately that's why the devil is primarily interested in this kind of evil—rather than just physical pain. It gives him more control.

A third truth contained in the Genesis account has to do with the concept of *relativism*. The Bible says that Adam and Eve fell from grace because they ate from the tree of the knowledge of good and evil. That sounds so innocent and harmless. After all, what's the big deal about eating some fruit? How could something so trivial possibly have such horrific consequences? And even if "fruit" were just a scriptural symbol for knowledge, what would be so terrible about that? After all, isn't learning good? Isn't truth good? Isn't knowledge about good and evil something that God wants us to have?

Yes, on all counts. But as I said in *Ten Prayers God Always Says Yes To*, Adam and Eve's desire to eat from the tree of the knowledge of good and evil did *not* mean that they were hungry to acquire knowledge. Nor did it mean they wanted to know the difference between good and evil. Those are huge misconceptions. They didn't care in the slightest about discovering the difference between right and wrong. They wanted to decide for themselves what was right and what was wrong. They wanted to reject God's law and make themselves the law. In other words, they wanted to usurp God's power and *be* God. That was their crime—the very same sin of the demons. And that's the truth that's being conveyed in the story.

We'll talk about the larger implications of this sin in a moment, but the immediate result was exactly what God said it would be: terrible suffering and death. In rejecting God, Adam and Eve lost everything that went along with being in union with God. They lost eternal life, they lost Heaven, and they lost the friendship of their Creator. And what they gained was not freedom or knowledge of any kind, but only exposure to the harsh elements of a fallen world: death, decay, war, sickness, corruption, loneliness, old age, and all the rest of the long catalog of human ills that have plagued mankind since time immemorial.

The bottom line is that the reason the world is such a mess today isn't because God is some kind of sadist who loves to inflict pain on his creatures. God didn't force us to reject him any more than he forced Satan and the demons to reject him. We did that ourselves, and we're still doing it today. That's the message of Adam and Eve.

Finally, the story of the fall of man teaches us an extremely important lesson about how the devil operates. And this is something we really need to focus on—because the invisible strategy employed by the devil in the Garden of Eden is the very same strategy he uses today. And it's one that continues to bear much fruit.

Satan, says Scripture, is a liar and the father of all lies. Understanding lying is the key to understanding the nature of the Evil One and the nature of spiritual warfare. Think about it. If God *is* Truth, and the devil hates everything about God, then naturally the devil is going to want to mess with the truth. What could be more offensive than to get us to act in a way that completely contradicts God's identity? What could be more insulting than for us to be persuaded to act in a way that is diametrically opposed to everything God stands for? That's why the devil is always trying to deceive us. Not only is it an extremely effective tactic for trapping us, but it also mocks God at the same time.

So deception is the foundation of all demonic strategy—it's the devil's modus operandi. And isn't it convenient for him that there are so many different types of lies? There are blatant falsehoods such as "God doesn't exist," or "There's no such thing as life after death." And then there are more subtle kinds of untruth, such as "You'll *never* be able to overcome that sin," or "You don't deserve to be happy," or "That person who just offended you did so for the most malicious motives, so it's all right to be angry."

The best way to lie is to mix some truth in with the falsehood. That makes the lie much more persuasive, doesn't it? For instance, a demon might suggest to an unsuspecting person, "It's not important to pray or read the Bible or go to church; the only thing that counts is being a 'nice' person." Well, yes, it's important to be a nice person. That's the true part of the lie. But it's also important to be nice to God! And a great way to do that is to pray and read the Bible and worship together on a regular basis.

It's so much easier to pull off a lie if part of it is true. Of course, it can be tricky to do this. You have to incorporate just the right amount of truth into your lie for it to work. If you add a bit too much or a bit too little, the person you're trying to deceive will likely see what you're doing, and the game will be up.

Well, the devil is an expert at this balancing act. He's been doing it for centuries, and he knows exactly how much truth he needs to feed us in order to get us to swallow his lies hook, line, and sinker. Take the example of Christmas. During that wonderful season of the year, the devil and his legions of demons have a great deal of success prowling through the world perpetuating one particular lie—a lie that always seems to work. You would think that it would be hard to get people to do the wrong thing, spiritually, at Christmastime. After all, everyone is being so nice to one another. Everyone is buying presents for their loved ones and laughing and joking and being kinder and friendlier than they usually are. You would think that Christmas would be the devil's "slow season."

Not at all! Satan is very smart. He knows that he's not going to be able to get good people to commit any really horrendous sins when they're in a happy state of mind and they're busy doing kindhearted things. So he doesn't even try. He doesn't try, for example, to convince a good person to kill someone or steal somebody else's money. That would be a waste of his time. So what does he do instead?

I'll tell you a little secret. The devil tempts good people to do good things. That's right. He uses what's good to snare us— especially at Christmas and other festive times of the year. The devil tries to get good people to do lots and lots and lots of good things. So many good things, in fact, that they neglect to do the *necessary* things—the things that are most important, such as praying and giving thanks to God and worshipping him. And that's exactly what happens at Christmas. People are so busy running around shopping for presents and buying food and going to parties and preparing meals that they hardly give a thought to the reason they're celebrating in the first place—the fact that God became one of us.

I'm not saying that all the hullabaloo at Christmas is bad. It's not. The lights and the music and the food and presents and the laughter are all wonderful. But that's exactly what the devil counts on. That's the "truth" that he mixes in with the lie—that we need to celebrate and do all kinds of special things because something special has taken place—the birth of Christ. The lie is that we need to do so many special things that there's no time to be prayerful and thankful and holy.

Satan loves trying to distort our sense of proportion in this way. It's such an easy lie for him to pull off. When he sees something that's legitimately "good," he doesn't try to convince us that it's bad. That wouldn't be intelligent. Instead, he goes the opposite route. He tries to make us think it's *so* good that we should be devoting every ounce of our strength to it. In other words, he tries to make us think a "good" thing is really the "most important" thing. And this is something he does all the time. He tempts some people to make food the most important thing in their lives. He tempts some people to make sex the most important thing in their lives. He tempts some people to make money the most important thing in their lives. He tempts some people with power, some with work, some with art, some with nature, some with worthy causes, some with their own devotion to their family. These are all good things, in and of themselves. But done at the wrong times or in the wrong degree, they can be disastrous to the state of your soul.

The point is, it doesn't really matter to the devil what's most important to *you*. The only thing he cares about is that it's *not* God. That's the focus of all his efforts: to separate you from God. He'll encourage any kind of indulgence—good, bad, or indifferent—as long as the main result is to skew your sense of proportion and distance you from the one source of true joy— your Creator. Remember, the first commandment given to Moses and the one that Christ identified as the most important is to love the Lord your God "with your whole heart, your whole mind, and your whole soul." If God is anything but number one in your life, then your priorities are screwed up—period. Knowing that, the devil's primary objective is always to get you to set up "false idols," and thereby relegate God to the number two position in your life—or number five, or number ten, or number fifty, or even better, get him off the list completely.

When you get right down to it, the devil doesn't really have a complicated strategy for winning souls. In fact, it's very simple. There are basically three kinds of beliefs or attitudes that he'd like every human being to adopt, three main "specials" on his diabolical menu. Let's take them one at a time.

First—atheism. There are many reasons that getting people to be atheists is at the top of the devil's to-do list. We could spend a long time talking about the centrality of faith and its importance to our salvation, but what I'd like to focus on now is something that is connected to faith in the most profound way: *repentance*. Faith and repentance are actually two sides of the same coin. True biblical repentance, like true faith, means turning toward God. It doesn't just mean believing in God's existence. After all, the devil believes in God's existence, too. No, faith and repentance mean *accepting* God, turning toward him, and embracing him with your whole heart and soul. Faith and repentence mean being sorry for your sins because you recognize that sin is a rejection of God.

This is such an important point. To be truly sorry for your sins implies that you have true faith, because you're turning toward God. However—and this is where the diabolical temptation comes in—unless you first believe in God's existence, you can't really repent for the sins you've committed against him; you can't really turn toward him in faith at all.

How does this work in practice? Let's say you've done a lot of sinning in your life. Let's say that, at one time or another, you've broken every rule in the book. In other words, let's say that you're like everybody else in the world! Well, God has an extremely lenient policy when it comes to rule breakers. All you have to do is confess from your heart that you're sorry and really try to change your ways, and you'll be forgiven. That's it! That's what "turning toward God in faith" means. That's the "good news" of the Gospels.

That's the whole reason that Christ died on a cross for us. Forgiveness is the very cornerstone of Christianity. God's name is Mercy.

That means that you can commit the same sin a thousand times, and if you're really, truly sorry, God is going to forgive you—*every single time*. The only thing that's absolutely necessary for that forgiveness to take place is that you *want* to be forgiven.

In other words, you have to be sorry, you have to repent, you have to want to amend your ways, you have to humble yourself and apologize to God.

Well, if you don't believe in God, then there isn't anyone to apologize to, is there?

And that's one of the reasons that the devil is so intent on encouraging widespread atheism. Over the centuries he has watched millions and millions of "deathbed confessions." He has watched millions and millions of people repent of their sins as old age and disease and tragedy have overtaken their lives. He has watched countless times as his hard work and effort to win a soul has gone up in smoke, all because the person decided at the final hour to simply say, "I'm sorry, Lord."

God's overpowering desire to forgive us is just too well known to humanity. It's all over the pages of the Gospel: the story of the shepherd and the lost sheep, the story of Mary Magdalene, the story of the adulteress who was about to be stoned, the stories of all those lepers and cripples and blind men who were healed of their bodily ailments, but whose sins were forgiven first. The most famous example is probably the story of the Good Thief—the criminal who was crucified alongside Christ and who asked, just before he died, if Jesus would "remember" him in Paradise. Well, Jesus didn't just say he would remember him; he said that the Good Thief would be *with* him that very day in Paradise. In other words, he proclaimed the criminal to be a saint—all because he turned to God in the final moments of his life.

The point I'm making is that the devil can read the Bible, too. He's not stupid. In fact, he's as knowledgeable about Scripture as the most erudite biblical scholar or the most passionate Baptist preacher. He knows the Good Book backward and forward, and he's very well aware of the doctrine of forgiveness. So when he goes about the business of temptation, he's extremely cognizant of the fact that the person he's tempting may thwart all his plans with a simple last-minute apology. Therefore his whole strategy must turn on something else—it must focus on efforts to ensure that the person he's tempting *doesn't repent in the first place*. And that's what atheism is perfect for, because, as we've noted, an atheist doesn't really have anyone to apologize to.

If that doesn't work, there's a second tactic the devil can use that's almost as effective as the first. If he can't get you to disbelieve in God, the next best thing is to try to make you disbelieve in God's mercy. This way of thinking and feeling is known as *despair*, and it basically says: "There may indeed be a God, but my sins are so terrible that he would never forgive me, so I might as well just keep doing what I'm doing, because I'm lost anyway."

This is an extraordinarily effective method of destroying souls, and one that's very easy for the devil to employ, since so many of us fall into the same sins over and over again. It's so simple to inject the idea into our heads that there's no hope; that it's pointless even to approach God because he's so disgusted with us—or so angry at us. Despite the well-known teaching on forgiveness that we have just spoken about, it's sometimes hard for us to believe that God is really as patient with us as he claims to be. After all, we're hardly ever patient with one another. Oh, maybe we'll forgive our neighbors a few times for the sins they commit against us, but we all know that if those neighbors keep repeating their offenses, they're out! Kaput! *Hasta la vista!*

That's why it's so easy to lose confidence in God's mercy. We have a tendency to judge him according to our own very poor standards, so of course we can't imagine that he would forgive us as many times as we sin. It just wouldn't be feasible because the number is so high. Not even God has that much patience! That's the lie the devil tries to perpetrate. And it's a terrible lie, because God *does* have that much patience, and he *will* forgive us, no matter how many times we fall.

But Satan is very smart. Not only does he encourage us to believe this lie; he also does his best to make us sin at those precise moments when the sinning will cause us the most discouragement. What do I mean? I remember when I was in my twenties and had just become committed again to my faith. I had not been a practicing Christian since my early teens, and now, as a result of meeting some wonderful people and reading some wonderful books, I was back to praying again and going to church regularly and working on my relationship with God. I was pretty excited. I had lived for years in a state of perpetual sin—mostly the kind that young, healthy Italian men like to indulge in—and now I was making an honest effort to live a holy life. And since I wasn't married at the time, that meant the A-word: abstinence.

That was *not* easy! Despite my newfound fervor, I continued to find myself chasing after girls and going to parties and falling into various kinds of debauchery, at least occasionally. I would feel sorry afterward—but I still did it. Now, here's the interesting thing. I began to notice a recurring pattern. I began to notice that it was after those times when I was feeling most spiritual—after I had been praying, or had attended church services, or had received communion—that I felt most tempted to go out and sin!

At first I thought this was just a coincidence. But then I realized that it couldn't be. It was happening too much. I'd be reading the Bible and praying up a storm and feeling like I had the courage of a martyr, and then I would go to church or a prayer meeting and happen to notice some pretty girls and that would be it. My thoughts would be in the gutter. Pretty soon I began to doubt the power of prayer. I began to question the value of worshipping God, even the benefit of receiving communion. After all, if these activities were so spiritually worthwhile, why weren't they helping me? If I could be singing and praising the Lord one minute and then practically running off to commit some sexual sin the next, what was the point? Maybe I just didn't have what it took to be a good Christian.

This kind of thinking began to seriously shake my faith. And that was the devil's mistake. Because he went a bit too far too fast, and I soon realized what was happening. It hit me one day that I was on the road to real spiritual despair, that I was losing hope in the possibility of my own salvation. And why should that be? Because I was twenty-four and had overactive hormones? Because I had some old habits I couldn't shake? Because I had only just started on the road to sanctity—a road that every spiritual writer in the world insists is long and arduous, a road that doesn't end until death itself—and I was already giving up hope? It was then that I realized that I was being duped. It was all a tactic. It was all a lie. Not my hormones, of course. They were very real. Not my inclination to sin. That was real, too. Both were part of being human.

No, the snare was the pattern of being strongly tempted to sin at certain very specific moments—in this case, immediately after I had prayed or worshipped—and the express purpose was to deflate my joy and destroy my faith. Once I figured this out (and it took me several years), I was never again tempted to despair. I was still tempted to sin, of course. But the sinning didn't discourage me as much—at least not to the point where I would ever dream of giving up my faith.

You see, *timing* is very much a part of the diabolical strategy. If the devil can get you to fall at the right time, in the right place, and for the right reasons, and if he can keep that pattern up long enough, the end result may be that you enter into a state of real hopelessness and despair. And when that happens, it doesn't matter whether you believe in God or not. You won't bother praying to him anymore. You won't bother worshipping him. You won't bother reaching out to him in times of suffering. Most important, you won't bother apologizing to him and turning to him in faith—even after you've sinned grievously, and even at the very end of your life. And that's just what the devil is after. That's his winning strategy—checkmate!

If both these methods fail, if the devil can't get you to disbelieve in either God's existence or his infinite mercy, there's one other highly effective tactic he can try. And I think it's his favorite tactic of all, because it weaves together all his other strategies and does so in an extremely elegant and seamless manner.

We talked a little before about the danger of having "false

idols," for example, money, food, sex, and so on. By far the worst idol we can have, though, is *ourselves*. I'm not just talking about an inordinate love of self. We all know how destructive that can be. Selfishness, self-absorption, and self-centeredness are qualities that invariably lead to loneliness and unhappiness. Most of us recognize that. What I'm talking about here is something even more dangerous because it's more insidious and more global in its nature.

What I'm talking about is the whole philosophy of humanist existentialism, a system of thinking that basically says that "man is the measure of all things," that there really is no such thing as objective truth, objective good and evil; and that the value of anything in life can be measured only by the subjective effect it has on the individual person, that is, *on me*.

In other words, what's good for you may not be good for me; and what's bad for you may not be bad for me; therefore, there is no such thing as truth. The only thing that counts is *how I feel*. The only thing that matters is *what I believe*. Basically, "it's my way or the highway."

Now, that's a very simplified definition of an enormously important and complex philosophy, but essentially that's what it means. And the most important thing to remember about this way of thinking is that the devil is its biggest proponent. The devil, in fact, is the quintessential humanist.

How so? Well, the devil would like it very much if we all believed we had the power to accomplish great things in life. He'd like it very much if we always "trusted in ourselves" and "relied on our own judgment" when making decisions. He wants us to believe in our hearts that we have the ability to be masters of our fate, and that we can become, in the words of the atheist philosopher Nietzsche, supermen and -women. In fact, the devil is always trying to encourage us to have confidence in "the power of the human spirit."

At first glance this might seem a bit confusing. After all, earlier in this book we were extolling the virtues of the human soul and talking all about how "God-like" human beings are and how wonderful it is that we have the power to create ourselves, overcome any kind of obstacles, and transcend the material world because of our invisible spirit. That's the Judeo-Christian position—and it's true. Yet we seem to be saying that the devil agrees with us! How can this be? Are we really on the same page with the Evil One? Does Satan really think that human beings are great and God-like?

Of course not! And this is where we come back to the diabolical strategy of mixing lies with the truth. The devil wants to deceive us, so what better way could there be than to frame his false argument in a way that resembles what we know to be true. Yes, the human spirit is special. Yes, we are made in the image and likeness of God. Yes, we have the power to forge our own destinies, regardless of the cards we've been dealt by genetics and our families and our environment. Yes, yes, yes. All of this is true.

But there's one little catch. When the devil encourages us to believe that we have the power to be "like God," he conveniently leaves out one essential detail—one detail that happens to be the cornerstone of all truth. And that detail is God himself.

The whole basis of humanist existentialism is that man can

do all kinds of marvelous, superhuman things *on his own*. According to this philosophy, man doesn't need anything or anyone, least of all God. In fact, God is seen as an obstacle to human achievement because of all the "unfair" restrictions he places on human freedom—all those annoying "Thou Shalt Nots." Remember how we said earlier that what happened in the Garden of Eden is still happening today? This is a perfect example. The serpent convinced Adam and Eve that they didn't need to obey God's laws concerning good and evil because they could make the laws themselves. They could be completely self-reliant and have anything and everything they wanted on their own terms and based on their own merits. According to the devil, *that's* the way for us to be "like God."

Only that's not the way. That's the kind of thinking that got us kicked out of the Paradise in the first place! That's the kind of thinking that brought death and suffering into the world. And that's the kind of thinking that saturates our society today. What do I mean? How familiar do the following statements sound?

I don't care what my parents say about living with my boyfriend. I'm going to do it anyway! I don't care what the Church says about abortion, it's my body and my choice, and I'll do what I want! I don't care what the Bible says about mercy, I won't forgive that person who hurt me so much! I don't care what Christianity says about helping the poor and the sick— I've got problems of my own and I've got to take care of myself first! I don't care about all that "loving your neighbor" stuff. My neighbor happens to be a royal pain in the neck, and I'll be as nasty to him as I please!

I don't care, I don't care, I don't care. I make the rules. I determine what's right and what's wrong. It's all relative, and I'm the only one who can decide what's true for me. I have the power to create myself and the world through my own choices, and I'm not going to let some book or some church or some "God" determine what's best for my life.

That's the philosophy of today, isn't it? And it's the very same philosophy that was taught by the serpent in the Garden of Eden, the very same philosophy that seduced our first parents. And it's all a lie.

The truth is that human beings *do* have the most extraordinary powers imaginable—but only when we act in *union* with God; only when we draw from *his* power operating *within* us. The Christian position is that God alone is all-mighty; God alone is all-knowing. Those are *his* qualities, not ours. And we have no right to claim for ourselves what doesn't belong to us. It's only when we unite ourselves to God that we can tap into that power and that knowledge and utilize those gifts in astounding ways. In fact, if we do that, then God himself—his very Spirit—will come and live inside us, elevating our souls and enabling us to be more like him. And it's when we become like God in this way that we can accomplish great things for his Kingdom.

That's the Christian meaning of being "God-like," and it's very different from the devil's distorted version. But do you realize what happens if we adopt his false way of thinking? For one thing, there won't ever be a reason for us to repent of our sins. There won't ever be a reason for us to turn to God in faith and contrition. Why? Because we won't believe that we have committed any sins to begin with! According to this philosophy, we're the ones who make up all the rules. So, of course, we're never going to be wrong. Why apologize to God then? Why turn to him at all?

And once again, the diabolical objective has been achieved.

The question is, how in the world can we ever win this battle when our enemies are so brilliant? It's so intimidating: the devil, the demons, their extraordinary intelligence, our own fallen human nature and our attraction to sin. What can we possibly do to fight against all this? Human beings are so puny and weak. If we can't even resist having that extra piece of cake for dessert, how can we ever have hope to combat such overwhelming forces?

Well, all I can say is, let's not give up hope quite so fast, because help is on the way. The kind of help I'm talking about is, like everything else we've discussed in this book, completely invisible. But it comes straight from Heaven, and I assure you it's more powerful than Satan and all his dirty little demons. You may have heard about it or read about it or even sung about it at church, but I'll wager you're not exactly sure what it means.

What is this strange form of divine help? Just an amazing little thing called *grace*.

CHAPTER 7

INVISIBLE GRACE

I remember once when I was seventeen or so and had just gotten my driver's license, I was on my way back home to Staten Island after a date in New Jersey and my car broke down. I had just gone over a little bridge, and before the engine cut out completely, I managed to pull off the first exit and roll onto some dark little street.

Now, this may not seem like a big deal, but at the time it was very frightening. I didn't know anything about fixing cars; I didn't have a clue where I was; it was late at night; I was all alone and didn't have a cell phone; and I had no idea what to do. I was just a kid. All kinds of thoughts ran through my head. What would happen to me? Would I be stuck there all night? Would I be robbed and killed by some vicious street thug?

Luckily for me there was a pay phone a couple of blocks away, and after I went rummaging through the car for some change (of course I didn't have any money on me), I ran over and called home. My father answered and I frantically explained the situation to him. The first thing he told me to do was to relax and not to worry. Then he asked me where I was, what the closest street sign said, and so on. He managed to figure out my exact location and told me to get back in the car and just wait; he would be there in twenty-five minutes.

I should mention that during the previous few weeks, I had been butting heads with my father over the usual things—work, school, my siblings, my sarcastic attitude, and so on. This seems to be a rite of passage for teenage boys, especially those who grow up in large Italian families with strong Italian fathers. I was at that stage where I seemed to be arguing with my dad over everything—this despite the fact that he had recently bought me the car I had wanted so badly. The car itself had been a major source of contention between us. It was very old and beat-up and had lots of mechanical problems—but it was a red convertible, and I really wanted it. He had reluctantly agreed to buy it for me, and now it had broken down.

None of this crossed my mind when I called him. All I knew was that I was scared and needed help. When I finally saw my father's car pull off the highway and come up behind me, I remember the tremendous feeling of relief. And when I saw him get out of the car, with his old green sweater with the holes in it that he wore when he watched TV at night, I remember thinking to myself that I was pretty lucky to have a father who would drop everything to come out and help me when I was in trouble—especially when I had been so difficult to deal with lately.

Looking back on it now, I realize that the predicament I was in is pretty similar to the predicament we're all in, all the time. My dilemma wasn't particularly huge. It didn't involve drugs or crime or death or anything like that. It was just a typical jam a teenager gets into. But to me it was terrifying; I had absolutely no resources, and I was powerless to help myself. I had no choice but to call my father. And he certainly didn't have to help me—at least not so willingly. I hadn't been acting like a respectful son, and I definitely wasn't grateful for all he had done for me. Yet, when he got my panicked phone call, he didn't hesitate to come and rescue me from my little ordeal.

It's the same for us. God created us out of nothing. We didn't bring ourselves into existence. He made us, gave us everything, and we rejected him. He is a good father but we haven't been very good sons and daughters. And now we find ourselves in a hostile universe, surrounded by spiritual forces that want to destroy us. And what power do we have to help ourselves? None. Absolutely none. After all, how can we hope to successfully combat the devil? How can we hope to achieve victory over an army of demons? How can we possibly resist all the seductive temptations of the world?

The answer is, we can't. We're really powerless. We don't have the resources. We don't have the intelligence. We don't have the strength of will. We don't have any of the capabilities that are necessary to overcome such overwhelming odds. Let's face it—despite all our potential, in the end we're just weak human beings. We need help. *A lot* of help.

Ultimately that's what grace is—help from God. And what's more, it's *unmerited* help. In other words, we haven't earned it. We can't win it. Yes, there are ways we can obtain it, and we'll discuss some of those in a moment, but, essentially, there's nothing we can ever do to *deserve* it. Grace is given to us freely by God, and it's given because of what Christ did for us in Jerusalem two thousand years ago.

His death on the cross is really the most incredible example of grace in history—our "redemption." When Adam and Eve rebelled against God, they did something so terrible that they could never make up for it on their own. That's a hard concept for us to understand, but it's true. If you do something wrong—such as lie to a stranger, for example—that's one thing. But if you lie to your boss at work, that's quite another. A lie like that might really get you in trouble. If you lie to a police officer, that would be even more serious. And if you lied to a judge in a courtroom after swearing an oath—that would have even greater consequences.

Or let's say that you had a spat with your neighbor, and maybe even threatened him or got into a fight with him. That might cause some commotion. But what if you tried the same thing with the president of the United States? What if you threatened him, or attempted to physically harm him? You'd be going to jail for a very long time, wouldn't you? You might even be shot by the Secret Service! The point is that the higher the position of the person you cross, the greater the consequences of the offense. That's just common sense.

Well, God is an *infinite* being. He has infinite powers, and we owe him infinite gratitude. After all, we owe him everything, including our lives. If we offend God, it's not just bad, it's infinitely bad. If we rebel against God, we've committed an infinite sin and therefore incurred an infinite penalty. That's exactly what Adam and Eve did.

The problem is that human beings are finite creatures. It's impossible for us to make up for an infinite sin. In order to do that, we'd have to be infinite in nature. Let me repeat that—only an infinite person can make up for an infinite sin. That's what justice demands. And that's why Christians believe that salvation comes only through Jesus Christ. As the second person of the

Trinity, Christ is fully God, so he satisfies the requirement of being infinite; yet he's also fully human, so he has the ability to make up for something *we* did. Thus, when Jesus lived a perfect life on earth and was perfectly obedient to his Father in Heaven— even to the point of dying on a cross—he was able to atone for Adam and Eve's sin of disobedience. That's the only way human beings could be forgiven. That's the only way they could be saved. Before Christ, human beings weren't allowed into Heaven. They had to wait. An infinite person had to atone for their infinite crime, first. There needed to be a second Adam—only this time Adam had to be God, too.

God not only created us, he also redeemed us and saved us through the actions of his Son. Even if you don't know who Jesus is or don't believe that he's God, that doesn't change what he did for us. And not only was this saving action done freely on his part, but it was done by him and him alone. We didn't do it ourselves—and we can't do it by ourselves today. Grace is, in its very essence, a gift—a gift that God continues to pour out in a million different ways. And the reason he continues to pour it out is because we continue to need it. After all, we still have free will. We still have the power to reject God if we want, and the devil knows it. As Saint Peter said, Satan is always prowling about the world, looking for souls to devour.

How does grace help us to keep from being devoured? Its purpose is to transform our lives so that we can function at an entirely new level—a much higher level. It's not really natural at all, but *supernatural*. In other words, grace involves the elevation of our natural abilities so that we can act more in accordance with the way God wants us to act.

Now, what does all that mean in plain language? Simply that it's very hard for us to live a good life, and God knows it! So in order to help us along, he's willing to give us a little nudge. Sometimes even a push. And this push comes in the form of divine assistance—assistance that has many benefits for us. Grace helps us, for example, to cope with life's difficulties; it fortifies us against temptations and helps us to get back on our feet when we fall; it helps us to be more charitable and merciful and joyful; it helps us to deal with problems on the job, problems in our families, problems in your own psychology; it strengthens our understanding of spiritual matters and helps us to defend our faith more vigorously and courageously; it helps us to be humble.

Sometimes God's help doesn't come directly from God. Although God is always the origin of grace, sometimes his help comes to us from other sources. It can come from an angel, for example. It can come from another human being who has been led to us by God. It can come from nature or music or even the movies. God has the option of using all of creation in order to move us in this direction or that. It's all grace.

But there's even more. Grace, at its deepest level, isn't just help *from* God—it's *God himself*. It's God living inside us. And it's this presence of the Holy Spirit inside our souls that transforms everything, permeates everything, and shapes everything we do. When grace is operating in our souls, it doesn't just mean that God is helping us to do certain things or to live in certain ways. It actually means that God is doing these things *himself*, and that he is involving us in the process. In other words, when grace is present in us, we're no longer the ones who are primarily doing the work. God is. Yes, he allows us to participate in that work in a real, substantive, and meaningful way, but it's still God who's the driving force.

What do I mean? Well, when a toddler is learning to walk, he can't do it unless someone practically holds him up and leads him by the hands. Yes, the toddler cooperates in the activity, by moving his hips and legs, and therefore he contributes to the activity of walking—he isn't simply being dragged along the floor. But in reality, we know that the person who is leading the child is the one who is doing the bulk of the work. It's the same for us. We're all babies in this world. We all need to be held up by the hands and guided along the right path in life. That's what God does for us in giving us his grace.

Now let me ask you a question. Do you think there's any value in God doing your work? Do you think that might affect the outcome? Do you think the chances of success would be greater if the Creator of the universe was the one who was doing the heavy lifting in your life? Of course! That's why it's so absurd when people set out to achieve all kinds of things—from making money to writing books; from finding husbands to conquering the world—and never once bother to ask for God's help, much less invite him to come live in their souls.

The most amazing thing is that when we cooperate with God in this manner, the end result is that *we* change. It is in the process of helping him do our work that we become transformed; that we become more like him. In the words of C. S. Lewis, we become "little Christs." This is a key point. Everyone in the world today seems to be searching for meaning, guidance, and order amidst the chaos of life. Well, what is God? As we said earlier, God is Peace. God is Wisdom. God is Order. God doesn't just have these qualities. He *is* them. He's identified with them. He's the source of them. So if God begins to live inside you in the form of invisible grace, and you begin to become more like him, what do you think is going to happen to your life? Doesn't it make sense that you'll become wiser? That order will be restored? That peace and calm will begin to reign in your soul? That you'll be guided in choosing the correct path to take? That you'll have more strength to do the tough things that are necessary for your life to improve? These are all the benefits that come from allowing yourself to be transformed by grace.

Sometimes people are afraid that if they give themselves over to God in this way, they might somehow lose their identity— they might somehow stop being who they are and instead become some kind of spiritual zombie or religious fanatic. Not at all! Not if you understand the kind of transformation I'm talking about. This kind of change doesn't result in any loss of self. On the contrary, when God's grace is operating inside us, we become *more* of who we already are.

You see, God doesn't want to turn us into different people. He doesn't want to give us this other person's gifts, or that other person's talents. Nor does he want to eradicate the good qualities we already have. Why would he? He's the one who gave them to us in the first place. The only traits God wants to eliminate are those that drag us down, those that enslave us and keep us from becoming who we're meant to be.

What God does want to do is to work with the gifts and talents we already possess—and those we don't even know we have—and add to them, until we become the equivalent of "super" versions of ourselves. That's what Aquinas and all the great theologians meant when they said that grace "builds on nature." When grace begins operating in us, we start to become the best possible people we can be.

What that means in practical terms is that if you have it in you to be funny, grace will make you funnier. If you have it in you to be analytical, grace will make you more analytical. If you're kind, grace will make you kinder. If you're creative, grace will make you more creative. Grace is all about actualizing, to a degree not humanly possible, all your God-given potential.

To illustrate this point, have you ever wondered why there are so many stained-glass windows in churches? Think about it. Without light, stained glass is very dull and dreary. On a rainy day or at night you can barely make out the stained-glass artwork. In fact, with its lead and metal framework, stained glass can be kind of ugly. But what happens the moment a ray of sunlight comes shining through? The image "hidden" in the darkened glass suddenly comes to life in the most extraordinary way. The stained-glass window is transformed into something beautiful and spectacular. Suddenly it's bursting with color. And not just any color, but the most vibrant, gleaming, wonderful colors imaginable.

Well, that's exactly what happens when the light of grace floods into the human soul. It's transformed. It's not changed into something alien. Instead, like a stained-glass window, it becomes what it's *meant to be*. And what it's meant to be is stunning and powerful and awe-inspiring. That's what grace does. It fulfills our potential completely.

Finally and most important, grace is the most powerful *life force* in the universe. We can't ever forget that God is Life.

Again, he doesn't just have life—he *is* Life. Moreover, he is Eternal Life. And that's precisely the kind of life he wants to give us. When God is inside us, in the form of invisible grace, eternal life is inside us. If you're afraid to die, you should meditate on that point for a while. Grace represents the beginning of eternal, everlasting life for you, *right now*. This isn't just a nice, poetic thought. It's reality. More than anything else, it's grace that puts us on the path to Heaven. Grace exists in the present moment, but its trajectory is eternal. You might say that grace represents the seeds of our life in Heaven beginning to blossom during our life on earth. It's amazing that in a culture so obsessed with health fads and diets and exercise and alternative medicine and all the hundreds of different ways of trying to prolong life, grace is so overlooked and neglected. After all, it's the only thing that can truly make us live forever.

And grace is not very hard to obtain, either. In fact, it's a lot cheaper than all those anti-aging products on the market! We've said that grace can't be earned or merited or won, but it can certainly be *accessed*. How so?

Very briefly, the way to "get grace" is through faith. Embracing faith wholeheartedly, turning away from sin and turning toward God by accepting the great gift that Christ has given us, is the fundamental way that grace will begin to operate in your soul. Connected closely to this is the Word of God. Sacred Scripture is a powerful form of God's presence, and it can always bring him to us if we read it prayerfully. Prayer itself is a tremendous conduit of grace. When we pray to God on a regular basis, we essentially open up a "communication channel" with the Almighty—a sort of "road" between Heaven and earth on which our thoughts, questions, pleadings, longings, joys, and sorrows can be sent *up*—and God's assistance, insights, inspirations, consolation, and miracles can be sent *down*.

Another way to access grace is through the community of believers. The Bible says clearly that "where two or three are gathered together in my name, I am there." It's so important that we stay connected to one another so that our spirituality doesn't get too individualistic and subjective. Staying close to the Church—to the "Body of Christ," as Saint Paul calls it—is like plugging our faith into a great generator in Heaven. It enriches our faith, it helps to keep us from falling into gross doctrinal errors, it inspires us, it encourages us, and it makes a tremendous difference in our lives.

Lastly, grace is communicated through what are commonly known as "sacraments." Sacraments are specific kinds of actions that bring the Lord's presence into our lives in a special way. Different faith traditions have different interpretations of how sacraments work, and it's not our purpose here to argue for or against any of them, but it's fair to say that most denominations within Christianity accept Baptism and the Lord's Supper as valid examples of this kind of grace-delivering action.

These are just a few of the ways we can experience God's invisible grace, but what's most important to get out of this discussion is the universal Christian teaching that grace is, without question, the most intense, dynamic, and powerful invisible reality in the world. When you're filled with it, anything can happen. When it's operating in your soul, there's no situation in life too big for you to handle, because there's no situation in life bigger than God.

And this leads us to a final observation we need to make before leaving this topic. Up until now we've treated grace as something that God gives us to help defend against the problems of life and the forces of evil. And that's very true, up to a point. But there's another way of looking at things. An even better way.

There's a famous scene in the Gospels in which the apostles tell Jesus all the things that people are saying about him throughout the region of Judea. Some people think he's the prophet Elijah; some think he's John the Baptist back from the dead. The apostles tell Jesus that everyone is amazed by his message and his miracles, but that no one seems to know quite what to make of him. When you read the passage, you can almost feel the apostles' giddiness as they relay this "gossip" about Jesus. And why shouldn't they be happy? After all, their master was becoming famous. He was shaking up society. But then Jesus turns the question back on the apostles by asking, "And who do *you* say that I am?"

After an awkward moment of silence, Simon finally speaks up and makes his great profession of faith: "You are the Christ," he declares, "the son of the living God." To which Jesus mysteriously replies: "Blessed are you, Simon son of Jonah, for this was not revealed to you by man, but by my Father in heaven. And I tell you that you are Peter, and upon this rock I will build my church—and the gates of hell will not prevail against it." Now Jesus was obviously saying several important things here. But it's the last part in particular that we need to focus on, because it has a great bearing on the whole subject of grace.

Christ said that he was going to found a church, and that

the gates of hell would not prevail against it. Let's think carefully about that phrase: *the gates of hell.* What does that mean? It's such a strange expression. After all, what are gates used for? What's their purpose? They're put up to protect things, aren't they? You put gates around your house, for example, or your property. You put them there so that intruders can't get in. In other words, when you install gates, it's primarily for defensive purposes. You're trying to keep something *out*, right? Something dangerous.

Well, then, what are "the gates of hell"?

What Christ meant was that there's a protective barrier that has been put up by the devil around hell and everything that hell stands for. There are gates around all the forces of evil. There are gates around the devil himself. There are gates around all the demons. There are gates around sin. But why? Why in the world would Satan have to put up gates? Why would he need to? After all, he's so powerful. He's so tough. He's so nasty!

The answer is that the devil has to put up gates for the same reasons we do: to keep intruders out. To protect himself and his domain from being attacked. And that's the fascinating thing about Christ's statement. He said the gates of hell would not prevail against us. But gates don't go out onto a battlefield and make war on anyone. They don't assault the enemy. In fact, they do just the opposite. They stay right where they are. Their job is to defend. So when Jesus told the apostles that the gates of hell would not prevail against his church, what he actually meant was that hell was going to be under siege. Hell was going to be attacked. Hell was going to need the gates to protect *itself.*

And guess who would be doing the attacking in this sce-
nario? Us! The community of believers. We're the ones who are
supposed to be storming the gates of hell!

According to Christ, hell is very much in the defensive position, while we're in the offensive position—not the other way
around. That puts things in a different light, doesn't it? Yes, it's
true that the devil is very powerful; yes, it's true that he hates
God and wants to destroy human beings. And, yes, he and his
demons spend a lot of time trying to tempt us to sin and discourage us. But the fact is that, in the overall scheme of history,
the devil and his demons are the ones who are on the run; *they're*
the ones who are losing; *they're* the ones who are afraid.

The best way to picture the battle between grace and sin
is to think of a fort in the middle of an open field. The fort is
occupied by Satan and his army of demons. Outside are the
people of God—average people like you and me, people who
believe in God and are trying their best to live good lives in
accordance with God's will. And we're attacking the fort. We're
trying to smash through the gates that protect it and turn the
whole structure into a mass of smoldering rubble. We're trying
to establish the Kingdom of God that we spoke of earlier, both
in this world and in eternity. *That's* the true picture of what's
happening in the invisible realm.

Now, those who occupy the fort aren't sitting idly by.
They're fighting back. Remember, they started the war in the
first place by rebelling against God and by trying to ruin all
those made in his image. But they were dealt a deathblow when
God became one of us in the person of Jesus Christ. That's the
historical fact that drove the demons into hiding and caused

them to seek shelter behind gates. And ever since then they've been fighting a losing battle; in fact, their only satisfaction has been to win as many souls as they can and offend God in the process.

In fact, that's their whole game plan. That's their war strategy. To offend God. And they're doing a pretty good job. The scary thing is, they have plenty of weapons behind those gates. They have missiles that they can fire at our universities, our political parties, our movie studios—even our churches. They have grenades they can lob at our newspapers and TV networks and big corporations. (And, of course, those are the places where they aim—they want to strike where they can influence the most people and do the most spiritual damage.) And they have demonic snipers, too, who can use their rifles to "pick off" as many individual souls as possible.

Sometimes the evil forces behind those gates have victorious days—sometimes even victorious years and decades; but the fact of the matter is that their fort is still doomed. Christ has already won the big victory, and he's already told us that in the end those gates—just like the Berlin Wall—are going to fall.

Despite the great power of the devil and his demons, *we're* still the ones who possess the heavy artillery. We're still the ones who have the benefit of grace. This amazing invisible force has the ability to vanquish the devil. It can blast huge, gaping holes through the devil's diabolical fortress and annihilate a whole battalion of demons. I'm not exaggerating one bit. Read any good book on moral theology or demonology and it will confirm exactly what the Bible says: in the presence of grace, evil flees, cowers, melts, and withers away into nothing.

Thérèse of Lisieux, an obscure little nun who lived in the late 1800s and died at the age of twenty-four, gained worldwide fame for holiness because of a book she wrote called *The Story of a Soul*. When she was just six or seven, she had a dream that illustrates the point I'm trying to make. She dreamed that she was alone in a strange, unfamiliar place—a garden of some kind. As she was walking around, exploring the quiet, deserted area, she suddenly had an eerie feeling that she was being watched. Looking over to a house nearby, she froze in terror as she saw the face of a demon staring out at her from behind a window. The face was horribly ugly, and Thérèse was about to scream and run away. But just as quickly as the demon's face appeared, it vanished beneath the windowsill.

The little girl was perplexed, and even though she was frightened, she crept slowly over to the house and peeked through the window. Inside she saw not one but two demons! One was squatting on a barrel, and the other was standing next to it. They were the most grotesque, evil-looking creatures she had ever seen. But then something very surprising happened. The demon who was squatting on a barrel suddenly saw Thérèse through the window and let out a terrible shriek. He immediately jumped onto the floor and raced to the door—as if he were trying to get away from her. The other demon had a shocked look on his face, too, and was desperately trying to hide from Thérèse by crawling into a hole in the ground. Thérèse, now amused, looked through the window at the two demons from hell and wondered why in the world they seemed to be so scared of *her*.

Years later, when she was older and more spiritually mature, Thérèse realized what the dream meant. She was sure God was teaching her about the power of grace. God was telling her that when someone is filled with grace, demons will flee in holy terror—even if that someone is a just little girl. Thérèse was just six or seven years old at the time, yet these evil creatures who had been alive for thousands of years, and had probably destroyed the souls of countless human beings, not only were powerless in her presence but were absolutely petrified by her.

And that's why Christ said the gates of hell would not prevail against us. That's why we're on the offensive—or at least we should be. The problem isn't that we don't have the ability to fight evil—it's that we don't use all the help we have at our disposal. We don't take advantage of grace. Many people don't even attempt to access it. And those of us who do don't always have confidence and faith in its power. It's as if we were fighting a battle with both hands tied behind our backs. No wonder we keep getting knocked down! G. K. Chesterton once said that Christianity "hasn't been tried and found wanting; it's been found difficult and left untried!"

It doesn't have to be that way. God has given us all the spiritual weapons we need, not only to defend against evil, but to triumph over it, to obliterate it. We've talked about only a few of these weapons in this chapter. But there are many more. In fact, there's one crucial one that we've left out completely. Outside of faith, itself, it might be the mightiest of all.

What is this secret weapon? Well, if we wanted to employ another military analogy, we might say it is as close to the "nuclear" option as we'll ever get in spiritual warfare. Indeed, that's exactly how the devil and his demons view it. It actually makes them tremble with fear. They're more terrified of it than they are of anything else in the heavenly arsenal. The funny thing is, it doesn't look like a weapon at all. In fact, to many people it looks just the opposite. It looks like defeat. It looks like collapse. It looks like failure. In fact, it looks very much like a cross.

CHAPTER 8

THE INVISIBLE POWER

OF SUFFERING

A couple of years ago I had dinner in Manhattan with two friends. One was an avowed atheist and the other an evangelical pastor. Both liked to argue, so I was looking forward to sitting back and being quiet while the two of them engaged in some friendly sparring. Sure enough, at some point between the appetizer and the pasta, the conversation got around to faith. The pastor asked my atheist friend if he ever wondered about the existence of God. My atheist friend responded: "No, I'm not a very spiritual person." To which the pastor shot back: "Well, you've got no choice; it's a spiritual world."

That was just the opening salvo in what proved to be an interesting evening. There was a lot of good conversation to come, but the one statement I've always remembered is: *You've got no choice; it's a spiritual world.* Many people don't seem to get this point. They may think they have a handle on things, but the truth is, they're missing out on a big piece of reality. In fact, they're missing out on reality itself.

It *is* a spiritual world we're living in, and to deny that is to live only half a life. Yes, you can pretend that the world is nothing more than millions of randomly moving molecules and that invisible spiritual forces don't exist, but you can't stop those invisible forces from affecting you. You can't stop the impact they're having on your life and the lives of your loved ones. In other words, you can ignore the invisible world as much as you want, but the invisible world is not going to ignore you!

The fact is that God exists, and he's invisible. And this invisible God created the angels, and they're invisible. And some of these angels—known as demons—decided to reject God, and they're invisible, too. And God created human beings, who have material bodies but invisible souls. And these human souls are very much hated by the demons, and as a result an invisible war for souls has been raging for thousands of years. And in order to help us win this war, God has given us an invisible form of help—known as grace.

To disbelieve these truths is to disbelieve the most important part of reality. Life isn't just what you see with your eyes. It's not just what you touch with your hands. The iceberg principle applies to everything in the world. So much that's real is under the surface. So much that's true is hidden and unseen. That's been the premise of this book up to now, and it's the context in which we're going to discuss one of the greatest of all mysteries—the mystery of suffering.

It's impossible to understand what suffering really is unless we first pull back the veil of human sorrow and look beyond the things we see and feel when we're in pain. When we do that we realize that there's a lot more to suffering than just that. There's a lot more that's invisible.

In order to make sense of suffering, we have to view it from a long-term perspective. In fact, we need to use the perspective of eternity. There's no other way to get at the truth. Remember, our souls are immortal. Human beings are meant to live forever. What happens to us today is going to affect how we act tomorrow, ten years from now, and fifty years from now. It's going to affect how we view the world and what's important to us and what kind of people we become. And these kinds of things don't just affect this life—they affect our life to come.

It's useless to try to judge the value of any human experience unless we take the next life into account. We simply can't say with any kind of certainty that just because something "hurts" that it's bad for us—at least not in the absolute sense. It may feel bad in the moment, but we know it might actually end up being something that benefits us in the long run, something that puts us on the path to Heaven. When it comes to suffering, things aren't black-and-white. Everything that happens to us in life—the pains, the pleasures, the joys, the miseries—all of it has to be viewed in the light of eternity.

Let's use an example from sports. One of the most famous and respected names in football is Vince Lombardi, the greatest coach in NFL history. Lombardi took a team of perpetual last place losers and turned them into champions. His teams won six titles in eight years, including the first two Super Bowls. He never had a losing season, and some of his wins—such as the infamous "Ice Bowl" victory—are considered among the greatest games ever played. Today, decades after his death, people still talk about him. His name is synonymous with winning, and, fittingly, the Super Bowl trophy is named after him.

Vince Lombardi was a great man, a man who got the most out of his players. But if you study the methods of this charismatic leader, you'll discover something very interesting: you'll see that he could be one of the meanest guys who ever lived! He was an extremely tough, demanding coach who never accepted less than a hundred percent from anyone around him—a man who put his players through a tremendous amount of hard work and, yes, pain.

And yet if you were to ask Lombardi's former players what they think of him, they would all tell you that they loved the guy; that he was a second father to them; that he was the single greatest influence on their lives; that he taught them how to be not only great football players but great human beings; that not a day goes by when they don't think about him and miss him.

How can that be? He was such a gruff, unyielding taskmaster. He was always yelling at his players. He was always putting them through excruciatingly painful drills, always pushing them beyond their limits. He never seemed to be satisfied. With Lombardi, there was no such thing as taking shortcuts or making excuses. It was all about hard work and single-minded purpose. The name of the game was to win—fairly and squarely, but to win.

In fact, Lombardi could be toughest on his team *after* a victory. If he felt his men hadn't played up to their potential or if they'd been the slightest bit lazy, he would be furious with them, and it didn't matter what the winning score was. That's because he was primarily concerned with the kind of people they were becoming. He didn't just want them to win this or that specific game. He wanted them to *be* champions. Winning was a mind-set, a way of life. He felt that if you had the guts to make it through the pain and strain and fatigue, you would emerge victorious in the end.

Yet all his men loved him. And they became champions. Why? In the final analysis, the reason that Vince Lombardi is still remembered today is because he understood one of the most important principles in life: Pain, if accepted in the right spirit, can help you. It can detach you from everything that's incidental and secondary in life and get you to focus like a laser beam on what's most essential. If used properly, it can lead you to ultimate victory—and ultimate happiness.

Now, of course, the game of life is a lot more important than any football contest. The stakes are infinitely higher, and the battle is incomparably harsher and more grueling. After all, the opposing team isn't made up of only big, burly men. It's made up of demons! And not just invisible spirits but our own "internal" demons as well—all our fears and phobias and weaknesses; all our inclinations toward pride and anger and lust and gluttony and laziness and avarice and greed. And these opponents don't ever stop. They're relentless. They never take a "time-out." They come at us night and day, when we're awake or asleep. They don't obey any rules, and they like nothing better than to kick us when we're down. Try fighting against *them* week after week. It's easy to get tackled!

Now, let me ask you a question. If life is tougher than football, and Heaven is more important than any Super Bowl victory, why should we expect God to be any less of a coach than Vince Lombardi? Why should we expect him to be any less demanding, driving, tolerant of laziness, or relentless in his pursuit of excellence? Why should we expect him to ignore the principle of "no pain, no gain" that has proved so effective in every field of human endeavor?

The fact is that God *can* be tough. Yes, he loves us. But it's not always a mushy, sappy love. Most times it's a tough love. A very tough love. The love of a good, strong coach—or a good, strong father. What we have to understand is that God isn't fooling around. Life is too short. Our enemies are too strong. Every day he tries his best to help us move a little closer to Heaven. And he'll stop at nothing to achieve that goal. *Nothing.* There's no cross too heavy that he won't make us carry, no fire too intense that he won't make us go through, if he knows the end result will be our salvation.

Please don't misunderstand me. I'm not trying to trivialize suffering. I'm not saying that cancer or death or poverty or any of the problems that make life so difficult are merely part of some divine "coaching strategy," and that all we need to do is "toughen up." Suffering is much more complicated than that, and the football analogy is far from perfect. The most important thing to remember is that God didn't *create* suffering. It wasn't part of his plan when he made the world. God isn't some twisted, sadistic puppeteer, dangling human beings by a string over a hot fire for his own pleasure. He's got better things to do than torture us. As we've seen, death and disease and disorder entered the world because of a choice that Adam and Eve freely made in the Garden of Eden. God hates suffering as much as we do. But he allows it because he never intended to create a race of emotionless, computerized robots. He wanted us to have the ability to possess true joy and happiness—the kind that he has. And the kind of joy and happiness he has is *free*. It's not forced. It's not mechanized. It's not just about pleasure.

Please understand this point. God could have made us robots

and put us right into Heaven. And we could have experienced all sorts of pleasure. But we would still have been robots. God didn't want that. He created us to be like him—free. He wants Heaven to be something we choose freely.

You see, what God really desires is a "love relationship" with us. And a love relationship can't be forced. It can't be imposed. You can have a love relationship only if both parties can freely choose *not* to be part of the relationship.

God didn't have to choose to create us. Likewise, he didn't want us to have to choose to love him or be with him. It all comes down to free will. Love, happiness, joy—they all must be freely chosen if they are to be experienced to the fullest possible degree. Unfortunately, the moment a person can make an authentically free choice, it's possible for that choice to be a bad one, a tragic one—a choice that causes suffering.

And that's exactly what happened in the Garden of Eden. At the very beginning of the human story, we went in the wrong direction. Ultimately, that's the reason that we inherited this crazy, tragic, beautiful world of ours, with all its potential for pleasure and pain. That's why life is so schizophrenic—unbearably happy one minute, unspeakably sad the next. It's all because of human freedom, and what that freedom resulted in.

The question from God's point of view was, once human beings made the wrong choice and rebelled against him, what could he do to help us? How could he allow us to exercise free will but at the same time bear the disastrous consequences we automatically incurred?

His solution, in a nutshell, was this: to permit suffering, but to *transform* it; to bring good out of it—more good, in fact, than would have been possible if Adam and Eve hadn't sinned in the first place. And this is the great "paradox of pain." Ultimately, the main reason God permits suffering is because he knows he can change it—somehow, in some way—into a greater good. That's really the crux of the whole theology of suffering.

Now, all this doesn't help us very much when we're going through a trial. Whether it's a toothache or unpaid bills or loneliness or grief, when we're experiencing pain, theology just isn't a big comfort. At such times we don't care very much about what happened in the Garden of Eden. We don't care very much that God didn't cause the pain. All we care about is that he's not fixing it! At those times all we really want is practical assistance. We want to keep things simple.

And that's why it's perfectly okay to think of God as a tough coach, or a loving but demanding father—one who's constantly driving us and pushing us to change—and to view all of life's challenges as pathways for God to enter into our struggles and transform them.

There's a story in the Gospels that always reminds me of this idea. It was late at night and the apostles were out on a little boat, crossing the Sea of Galilee to a place called Gennesaret. Jesus wasn't with them—as usual he had stayed behind to pray. Anyway, it started to storm. The boat was tossed up and down on the waves, and it was thundering and raining and the wind was howling. Just then a bolt of lightning lit up the black sky, and the apostles saw, to their amazement, a man walking toward them on the water. They were terrified. They thought it was a ghost!

Imagine how eerie the scene must have been, with darkness

enveloping everything, and every few seconds flashes of lightning illuminating this ghastly white figure gliding slowly over the water, his robes blowing in the wind! Of course they were scared. It was like a scene out of a horror movie. But out of the darkness they suddenly heard the man on the water yell out to them: *Take courage! It is I. Don't be afraid.* It was only then that they realized it was Jesus.

This story has always fascinated me. Why in the world would Jesus have gone out walking on the water in the middle of the night during a thunderstorm? What was his motive? He must have realized the effect it was going to have. He must have known he was going to scare the daylights out of the apostles. Obviously that was part of his plan. Obviously he wanted to teach them—and us—a lesson. He wanted to say very clearly that when scary things happen to us—when it's storming in our lives, when we're in the midst of darkness and troubles and anxieties and pain—that we always have to remember not to worry because *it's really God*. He's right there with us. He may not be the direct cause of the pain, but he's in control of the ultimate outcome of our suffering.

This is a hard teaching, I know, and it's one that's very likely to get you angry at God—especially if the pain you happen to be experiencing is severe. But God is pretty sturdy. He can take your being upset with him or even beating up on him once in a while. What's most important to him is that you make it through the hard times in life with your peace of mind and faith intact. And the only way to do that is to believe in your heart that, no matter how minuscule or how terrible the suffering, God is in control. Whether it's cancer, money problems, or the death of someone you love—God is there, coming to you in the darkness, just as he came to the apostles that stormy night two thousand years ago. And he's saying the very same thing to you that he said to them: It's okay. It's me. I know this is a scary experience, but try not to worry. In the end, everything is going to work out exactly the way it's supposed to. I'm going to take this terrible thing that's happening and use it to achieve something meaningful. Something greater. Just trust me. *Don't be afraid.*

Sometimes it's easy to see what that greater good is; sometimes it's not, especially when death is involved. But those are the times when you have to trust God the most. Those are the times you just have to accept on faith that he sees more than you see—that he sees both the visible and the invisible; that he sees into the future and even beyond, into eternity; and that he knows what's best for you, and for the person who died, and for your family and friends, and for the whole world. That's what faith in God is all about: trusting even when you can't see with your eyes or understand with your mind. Remember, Christ never said, "Blessed are those who understand." He said, "Take up your cross, and follow me."

Is that hard to do? Yes! Brutally hard. Nobody likes crosses. Nobody likes to suffer. But oftentimes that's exactly what we need most, because that's what *works best*. In the end, it's the crosses and trials and tests that are most effective in shaping us into the kind of human beings we're meant to be. Crosses *change* us. They change us by exposing the invisible truth about life— the truth that the devil wants to keep secret from you, the truth that the devil wants to stay hidden—the truth that we're in the midst of a colossal invisible battle.

Crosses change us by ripping away all the nonsense and triviality and vanity and shallowness that surround us, and showing us the things that are truly important—the things that concern God. And this knowledge, if it sticks, has the power to change us forever. Mark my words, if you're suffering in any way right now, one of the reasons God is permitting it is because he wants you to change.

My goodness, when I'm honest with myself about my own character flaws—and there are many—I cringe at the thought of how I might have turned out if I hadn't gone through some of the more difficult experiences of my life. Can't you say the same? Look back at your own life and see if it wasn't the really painful experiences that caused you to grow and mature the most as a human being. By the same token, look at the things in your life that you're proud and happy about now, and see if they didn't come about as a result of the setbacks you had, and because of the hard, exhausting efforts you made to combat those setbacks.

This is true of practically everything in life. You've heard the old example. If you leave a piece of black, sooty coal alone, it stays a piece of black, sooty coal. But if you put it under intense pressure, it becomes a diamond. Likewise if you want to improve yourself in any area, you have to be put under intense pressure. Whether you're trying to increase your strength or your memory or your patience or your ability to play the piano, you always need to be pushed, challenged, and tested. You have to be willing to pay the price. And the price, unfortunately, is pain.

The same goes for whole societies. Orson Welles had a great line about this. He said, "In Italy, for a period of thirty years in the fifteenth century, they had warfare, terror, murder, and bloodshed—and yet they produced Michelangelo, Leonardo da Vinci, and the Renaissance. In Switzerland, for a period of five hundred years, they had brotherly love, democracy and peace—and what did they produce? The cuckoo clock!"

Now, of course, I'm not advocating war. But there's no denying that great suffering often results in great advances and even great benefits to mankind. The reason is that suffering detaches us from ourselves and frees us to help others in a totally selfless way. Moreover, it forces us to become attached to God. You see, each of us has a built-in mechanism of "self-reliance." And it's false. It's completely artificial. Apart from God, human beings can't do anything. We're just weak, fallen, sinful creatures. No matter how rich or successful we become, it can all go up in smoke in a second. One bad phone call from the doctor is all that's required to end our false conceit. Yet we continue to have this enormously stubborn will. We want to do what *we* want to do. And we want to do it *now*. It has been that way ever since the beginning of time. Pain is the only thing that really has the power to disable that stubborn will; it's the only thing that makes us realize how dependent upon God we truly are for every breath we take.

The interesting thing is that when our self-reliance finally begins to die and we start relying on God, there's no limit to the amazing kinds of feats we can perform. This is the other great paradox of life. Christ said: "Unless a grain of wheat falls into the earth and dies, it remains alone; but if it dies, it bears much fruit." And it's true. Think about it. If you want to be a thin, fit, energetic person, then your overweight, lazy "self" has to die. If you want to be a good, faithful husband, then your lying, adulterous "self" has to die. If you want to be a humble, virtuous person, then your prideful, willful "self" has to die.

I once heard a pastor say that if a mineral could desire to be a plant, it would have to cease being a mineral first. Its mineral nature would essentially have to give way to something new— something higher. In the same way, if a plant wanted to be an animal, it would have to give up being a plant. And if an animal wanted to be a human being, it would have to first relinquish its animal nature. The very same is true for us. We're all called to live a higher kind of spiritual life. We're all called to live in the Kingdom of God. In order to do that, we have to be willing to give up our purely human nature. We have to be willing to "die to ourselves." The old self has to be willing to give way to the new self. That's what practicing Christianity is all about. That's what suffering is all about—dying to ourselves.

Unfortunately "dying" is a painful process! But if we're able to do it with faith and trust, there's no telling what kind of miracles will result. And this is the final point I'd like to discuss: the fact that sacrificial suffering is the most powerful spiritual weapon on the face of the earth. When it comes to combating the forces of evil, there's really nothing that compares to it.

We have to remember that when Christ accomplished our redemption, he didn't do it by giving a speech, or writing a book, or donating money, or shouting from the hilltops about love and tolerance. He did it by being nailed to a cross and dying a painful death. That's the method he chose to overcome evil. That's the method he chose, in fact, to overcome death itself.

Well, God knows what he's doing. He knows what works and what doesn't work. And suffering works. During his passion, Christ experienced every kind of suffering imaginable. He suffered humiliation and embarrassment, mental anguish and emotional stress, sorrow and loneliness and depression; he suffered searing physical pain throughout his entire body, from his feet to his legs to his back to his chest to his hands to all his joints. The crown of thorns digging into his scalp felt as painful as any migraine headache, and the horrible suffocating sensation he felt hanging on the cross was as bad as any respiratory ailment. He went through it all. And in some mysterious way, when he cried out to Heaven: "My God, my God, why have you abandoned me?" he even experienced the nothingness and emptiness and black hopelessness of the unbeliever. At that moment, it can actually be said that God himself felt something of what it's like to be an atheist. Yes, Christ even went through *that*.

Why did he endure so much? For the simple reason that he wanted to unite himself to us. He wanted to *feel our pain* in the same way that we feel it. By experiencing all the different kinds of anguish that we go through, Christ gave meaning to human suffering. Before Christ, all suffering was worthless. On a purely natural level, it may have helped people to grow and mature (as it still does today), but it had no spiritual value whatsoever. When Christ used suffering to save the world, he transformed it into a weapon to combat evil. It's because Christ united himself to our suffering that we can now unite our suffering *to him* and use it to help others.

Saint Paul said in his letter to the Colossians: *"I fill up in my Flesh what is still lacking in regard to Christ's afflictions, for the sake of his body, which is the church."* This has always been a hard scriptural passage for people to understand. Paul didn't mean that

God needs our help in any way—he doesn't. Our salvation is a free, unmerited gift, and none of us can add to it or detract from it one iota. But at the same time, God wants to give us a chance to help the people around us in the same way that he saved the world—*through suffering*. That's what we mean when we say suffering has a "redemptive" value.

Now, there are lots of ways we can help people. We can pray, we can fast, we can give money to the poor, and we can contribute our time and effort to worthwhile causes. And all of these are good things to do. But the truth is, none of them is as powerful as redemptive suffering. None of them is as effective as saying, "God, I feel horrible right now, but I want to offer up my suffering for the sake of that person over there."

Why? Because when you accept the suffering that comes to you from God in a trusting, faithful way, you're doing something that's totally contrary to the philosophy of the world and the devil. You're acting in a purely selfless manner. In other words, you're being Christ-like.

In practical terms, what this means is that every single time you experience pain, you can "attach it to the cross" and unite it to the sufferings of Christ. There is immense spiritual value in this. It means that if you have a backache, you can offer it up to God and affect the life of someone on the other side of the planet. If you're depressed, you can offer it up and help your son or daughter through a crisis they might be having. If you're stressed out, you can offer it up and bring a coworker back to the faith. If you have cancer, you can offer it up and help save someone's eternal soul. This is not spiritual rhetoric. This is *literally* true.

Redemptive suffering is the most powerful form of intercessory prayer.

And redemptive suffering isn't just useful to those who are alive now. It can be employed by God to help people who haven't even been born yet. Remember, God exists outside time and space. For him there is no past or future. There's only the eternal present. So when you unite your sufferings to him, these people, too, begin to exist outside time and space. They, too, become "eternally present." Therefore it's possible not only to pray for future generations, but also to offer up your suffering for them. It's a concept that boggles the mind, but if you think about it, it makes perfect sense.

Let me illustrate this point with a story from my own family history. It has to do with my grandmother on my father's side, Elisa Pesiri, who came to this country from Italy when she was just twenty years old.

My grandmother, whom I never met, had a very hard life; in fact, her story might almost be an Italian version of *Angela's Ashes*. She left her little mountain town near Naples for the same reason that so many other immigrants did: there was nothing there for her except poverty. She came to New York on a steamship with her cousin, who was also twenty years old. Can you imagine that? Two girls barely out of their teens coming to a strange country alone. And it was wintertime. They spent Christmas and New Year's Eve on the boat before arriving at Ellis Island. I've often thought about how it must have been for them on that bitterly cold voyage across the Atlantic. There must have been some sort of Christmas celebration, with

Italian singing and some food and everyone huddled together for warmth. But I'm sure they were frightened.

Anyway, they got to Brooklyn and started their lives here. My grandmother had the misfortune to marry a real worthless character, a violin-playing, philandering shoemaker who treated her horribly and abused her for many years. At some point he left her, but not before she had eleven of his children. Eleven! He left them all, flat broke with basically no means of survival. He was a real piece of work, my grandfather.

To add to this, one of the children—a little boy—died of diphtheria when he was just three. Then a year later one of the girls died from another illness. The only thing that made all the suffering bearable for my grandmother—aside from her strong faith in God—was the presence of her oldest son, Carmine, who was, by all accounts, a little saint. He went to school during the day and worked at night, and he gave everything he earned to his mother. He was a responsible, dutiful son, and he tried hard to be the "man" of the family. Of course, my grandmother loved him very much. But like all the young men of his generation, he was eventually drafted into the service and had to leave home. I have some of the letters he wrote during the time he was in the army. They're quite poignant. All of them are full of anxiety for his mother and brothers and sisters. He was always worried about the kids playing on the fire escape, or fighting too much, or having enough to eat.

Then the big blow struck. After just sixteen months in the army, Carmine was inexplicably sent home. At first everyone was happy. Then they learned why: he had leukemia. Within a year he was dead. He was only twenty-two. You can imagine the pain my grandmother must have gone through. From what I understand, she wanted to die. But for the sake of her other children, she somehow managed to go on. Every Sunday, without fail, she would go to the cemetery to visit Carmine. It didn't matter if it was raining or snowing, scorching hot or freezing cold—she would get on a bus and go to the cemetery to pray at the grave of her beloved son. Sometimes she would take one of her other children to accompany her. According to my father, who was just a little boy at the time and who made many such trips with her, she didn't say much on those bus rides. She just sat there, dressed in black, praying silently. In fact, despite all the hardships she endured in her life, Elisa never stopped praying, never stopped going to church, never stopped believing. Nor did she ever once curse God for her fate. She just suffered quietly and with faith.

And things didn't get any easier for her. Raising eight kids in a small Brooklyn tenement building without a husband was hard. The kids were wild. They argued and fought all the time. When things got out of control, she would bang her head against the wall and moan over and over in Italian, *Dio, pigliami*—God take me! That would finally get their attention and they would gather round her and beg her to stop.

One day when my father was seventeen years old, he was out playing stickball on the street in a nearby neighborhood when someone called out to him from one of the apartment building windows that his mother had been rushed to the hospital. He dropped his stick and ran twelve blocks to the hospital, sweating and panting. My grandmother had had a massive stroke due to high blood pressure. But there was nothing anyone could do.

She died at fifty-five years old and was buried just a few days before Mother's Day. It was quite a scene—all those grief-stricken children gathered around their mother's coffin in the cemetery, crying. Like something out of a Dostoyevsky novel. On Mother's Day they all went back again, and the mound of dirt on her grave was still brown and fresh.

My grandmother's death was devastating for the children. The whole family scattered and many of them lost their faith. My father, in particular, couldn't understand why God would do such a thing to a woman who was so good, and who had suffered already so much. For the next thirty years he stayed away from church. He rarely prayed, and he basically led a hedonistic lifestyle. Eventually he got married and had five children, of whom I was the first. Because of his apathetic attitude toward the faith, none of us grew up being "religious." We hardly ever went to church, we didn't attend parochial school, and we didn't read the Bible or pray together. We didn't do anything that could be construed as spiritual. We were Christians in name only; we were well on the road to becoming typical of so many people without faith.

Then something very interesting happened. My younger sister, for some strange reason, started praying. She did this on her own. Neither my parents nor any of our relatives or friends told her to do it. In fact, no one even knew about it. It was her secret. She just got it into her head that she wanted to be close to God. In fact, she became quite the spiritual little girl. She started praying for all of us. She started reading the Bible. She started getting up early in the morning to listen to Christian radio. After a few years she became intensely spiritual. So much so that she even managed to get me interested in what she was doing. Before long I found myself reading the Bible and praying and going to church. Then my brother started doing the same. Then another brother. Then another. Then one of those brothers decided to become, of all things, a priest! And I started writing, of all things, spiritual books! Spiritual books that have been published (believe it or not) in almost every country of the world. Somewhere along the line, even my father, who had been away from the faith for decades, started going to church again.

It was an amazing thing to watch. And it all came about as a result of my sister—whose name, by the way, just happens to be Elisa.

The question is: Why? Why did it happen? I could understand it if one or two of my siblings became faithful Christians despite our secular upbringing. But the whole family? And in such a powerful way? It just doesn't make sense.

For me, the explanation lies with my grandmother. I can't prove it, of course, but I think that my family's return to the faith was a direct result of my grandmother's faithful suffering, suffering that she offered up to God every day of her life. No one really saw it at the time, but she lived a very Christ-like existence. From the time she was on that steamship, lonely and afraid, to the miserable years she spent with her abusive husband, to the unbelievable pain she went through when her children died, to her last agony in the hospital, that woman never left Calvary. Her whole life was a slow, grueling crucifixion, which she endured with heroic faith and trust. And even though she didn't realize it then, the pain that she bore so patiently had incredible spiritual power. So much power, in fact, that it was able to reach into the next generation and radically alter the lives of our whole family.

As I said, I can't prove it, but I believe it. I believe that because one poor, uneducated immigrant woman offered up her prayers and her pain to God fifty years ago, a chain of invisible events was put into effect that began with my sister secretly praying and eventually led to your reading these words right now. Who knows where it will end?

The point I'm trying to make is that suffering doesn't have to be meaningless. It can be profoundly important, not only for you, but for your children and grandchildren. Look, we all know that there's no amount of money or success or influence that can ever prevent pain from entering our lives. It's going to happen, sooner or later. The question is, when it does, how are you going to react? When you experience adversity or failure or humiliation or physical pain or sadness, what are you going to do? Are you going to become angry and disillusioned? Are you going to lose your faith? Are you going to turn inward and live such a guarded, cold, and defensive life that there's no chance that you'll ever be happy?

Or are you going to do something else? Are you going to try to believe that there's more to your pain than meets the eye? Are you going to try to believe that there's an invisible power in your suffering? Despite the storm raging around you, are you going to try to see God walking toward you, and listen to his voice crying out to you in the darkness:

Take courage! It is I, the Lord. Don't be afraid!

CHAPTER 9

INVISIBLE DESTINY

Death, Judgment, Heaven, and Hell

A ll the invisible realities we've been discussing so far have been leading up to one subject. It's perhaps the most fascinating subject in this book—because it affects each of us so personally. It's also a subject that's very misunderstood. It has to do with our ultimate destiny. It has to do with what happens to us at the very end of our lives on earth. In other words, it has to do with the subject of death and the invisible realities that await us beyond the grave.

I remember the first time I thought about dying—I mean *really* thought about it. I must have been sixteen or so. I think it was a weekend, and as usual I was up late after everyone in my family had gone to sleep. I was in the living room on the couch, and I had just turned out the lights after finishing reading. It was completely dark in the room except for the blue digital time display on the video player. For some reason I started staring at those little blue numbers, waiting for the time to change. When you do that for a long time without blinking your eyes and the room is already dark, everything seems to get even darker and fuzzier; and if you're tired, you can go into a kind of trance. I was in that sort of a state when, for whatever reason, I started thinking about death. I don't remember what the chain of thoughts was that led me to the subject, but for the first time in my life I actually tried to picture myself dead.

Now, I should tell you that normally I'm a very cheerful person, and back then especially so; I was always laughing and joking around and never gloomy. But this one time, I allowed myself to indulge in morbid thoughts. I imagined myself in a coffin, lying there dead, wearing a suit, my face all pasty with makeup. Then I pictured the coffin in a grave, with me in it under the ground. I imagined my body undergoing decomposition, and the odor that would result—the odor coming *from me*. Then I pictured the skeleton that would eventually be the only thing left—*my skeleton*. I pictured all the gory, grotesque details. I didn't spare myself one bit. (Sixteen-year-old boys can be pretty disgusting!)

Then I imagined what it would actually feel like to be dead. Not sleeping. Not unconscious. But dead. I tried to imagine the silence, the stillness, the emptiness, the nothingness. I really worked myself up. Then, finally, I thought about the fact that this wasn't just a fantasy of mine, but reality. This was *definitely* going to happen, and there was no way my father or mother or anybody in the world could stop it. Someday I was actually going to die—me—Anthony DeStefano—with all my thoughts and feelings and memories and hopes and talents and desires and ambitions and good qualities and bad qualities. I would be dead and buried. It seemed too terrible to believe.

I imagined it all as clearly and vividly as if it had happened already, and at some point I actually let out a shriek and leapt up from the couch and turned on all the lights in the living room. Not just the lamp next to me, but every single light I could find. I lit up the whole place. Then I went into the kitchen, got some soda out of the refrigerator, made myself a sandwich, came back into the living room, and turned on the TV. Then everything was all right again. Then I felt okay.

Anyway, that was how I dealt with the awareness of my own mortality the first time it hit me. Now, I know this isn't very original—countless people have felt the same thing. But I relate it here because so many people think about death the wrong way. They think of it exactly the way I did when I was sixteen. They think of it as black nothingness. As total annihilation. They picture the stillness and silence of the tomb, and they imagine that the person who's dead is also still and silent. They believe all that because that's what they see with their eyes. That's what's visible to them. But as we've said so many times in this book, there's a lot more to reality than what our senses can detect. In fact, the idea that death represents the end of all thinking and knowing and caring and being is the opposite of the truth. It's completely contrary to what Christianity teaches. According to most central doctrines of the faith, the moment of death is not quiet or still at all. It's a time of extraordinary activity. In fact, it's probably the *busiest* moment of our lives.

When a person dies, there's not a single solitary second when he feels "nothing." The whole period of "passing over" from the old life to the new is seamless and instantaneous. God doesn't allow you to skip a beat. Yes, your body may be dead, and your friends and family may be standing around you, looking down, sobbing silently, and reflecting on the mystery of life and the finality of death, and other such solemn topics—but to you, the person lying there, the reality is much different.

At the very moment you die, your soul is liberated from your body. And your soul remains very much *alive*. It doesn't die. Remember, the human soul has a beginning but no end. It was created by God to be immortal. As we've said earlier, the soul is the "animating principle" of your body. In other words, it's the very force that gives you life, that makes your body breathe and move. So when it leaves the body—when it "shuffles off this mortal coil," as Shakespeare said—it has no problem existing on its own, because that's its natural state: to live.

Now, what, exactly, will that moment of death be like? What kind of invisible things will be happening? Well, when the separation of the body and the soul occurs, it's important to remember that you will still be *you*. Your identity—everything that makes you the person you are—will remain intact. You'll have awareness. You'll definitely know who you are and what has happened to you. You're not going to suddenly get amnesia in the afterlife! This is one of the biggest differences between Christianity and Buddhism and other eastern religions. According to those faith traditions, people really don't have any kind of permanent "identity." They believe that when you die, whoever you were in this life ceases to exist. Yes, your spirit may continue on in other ways and forms, but it won't be *you*. Christianity teaches the exact opposite: in the next life, not only will you continue to be yourself, but you'll actually become *more* of who you really are. Your true personality—your "best" you—is what lives on in Heaven.

Another thing Christians believe is that when you die, you'll be able to see. Not with your eyes, of course, but with your soul, with your intellect. How is that possible? Well, angels can "see" and they don't have eyes. God can "see" and he doesn't have eyes. And you, yourself, can "see" when you're dreaming and your eyes are closed. That's because when you're sleeping you can still "look" at things with your mind. It's the same principle at work here. Your soul doesn't need your eyes to see. Sight is a power that comes from God. It so happens that when you're alive and have a body, the seeing mechanism is carried out through your physical senses—through the optic nerve and retina and pupil and cornea and iris. But that whole filtering process actually slows down your vision. When your soul is separated from your body, there won't be any such physiological limitations. Your ability to see will be much more powerful because it will be unhampered and unrestricted.

Nor will you be alone when you die—because your guardian angel will be there with you. As we discussed earlier, an angel was specially given to you by God at the moment you were conceived in your mother's womb, and this angel has been at your side ever since. He has been standing right next to you during every important event of your life, and he has helped you countless times, even though you may never have known it. The whole purpose of his mission has been to assist you with the ups and downs of life and to help you make it to Heaven. Does it make any sense that he would abandon you at the very end? Of course not. He's going to be right there with you. And even though he's a pure spirit, in some mysterious way you'll be able to see him, know him, communicate with him, and recognize the role he has played in your life.

This "recognition" of things as they truly are is one of the most important features of the afterlife. Many people are afraid that when they die, they're going to be immersed in darkness. After all, when you close your eyes, it's dark. But again, this is the very opposite of the truth. According to the Bible and to every faith tradition within Christianity, God is *Light*. And his Kingdom is a Kingdom of Light. When you die, you're not going to be suddenly plunged into some kind of black hole. Death doesn't resemble sleep or unconsciousness at all. It's nothing like nighttime. It's nothing like being in a dark room—or a dark coffin. The very instant you die, you're going to be bathed in God's light. And that light is bright and beautiful and warm and inviting.

Moreover it's a light that illuminates all of reality. Everything that was previously hidden from you—the whole invisible world that we've been speaking about—will suddenly come to life in crystal-clear, magnificent Technicolor. You'll become clear, as well. For the first time you'll be able to see the invisible truth about yourself. You'll see yourself as you really are—as God sees you. You'll see the good, the bad, and the ugly. You'll see how much of your life was given over to love, and how much was given over to vanity and selfishness. You'll see for the first time the true horror of sin, and what it has done to disfigure the universe as well as your own soul. You'll see it all in one moment, because it will be lit up by God's all-illuminating light.

In fact, it's this light that constitutes the essence of what Christians call "judgment." Many people misunderstand the concept of judgment. They think it means that when you die,

God is going to be waiting for you at the pearly gates with a big baseball bat in his hands, ready to bop you over the head for all the sins you committed! As if God didn't have better things to do! No, judgment is something that, for the most part, comes about automatically. And it's something that we basically do ourselves. Let me explain.

When a person rebels against God, there's a natural, built-in consequence. Sort of like when you put your hand in a fire. When you do that, you get burned—immediately. There's nothing that happens in between. No other process is required before you feel the burning sensation. Your brain doesn't have to make any decisions. Getting burned occurs as a consequence of your action. It's the same if you jump in the water. A natural consequence of that action is that you're going to get wet. It's just automatic. Likewise, if you leave your nice warm house in the middle of the wintertime and don't wear a coat, you're going to feel cold. It just happens as an automatic consequence of something you did. Nothing can me more simple, right?

Well, something similar occurs when you sin. Anytime you rebel against God—and that's exactly what sinning is, rebelling against God—there's a natural consequence, a built-in, automatic result. And that result can basically be described as *disorder*. Remember, God is Peace. God is Order. Any revolt against him is going to result in disharmony and disorder. And this disorder must necessarily cause—at some point in time—pain and unhappiness.

Please understand, God doesn't have to *do anything* to make you feel that pain. He doesn't have to "punish" you. He doesn't have to send a single thunderbolt down from Heaven. The pain you experience is a built-in consequence of abusing your free will. When you rebel against God, there are natural consequences that are going to follow—every single time. Just like putting your hand in the fire or jumping in the water or leaving your house without a coat on a wintry day. It's a law of the universe every bit as certain as gravity.

Why? Because if you turn away from God, you're essentially turning away from everything that God is. That means that since God is Light, turning away from him means plunging into darkness. Since God is Order, turning away from him is going to result in chaos. Since God is Peace, turning away from him is going to cause strife. Since God is Beauty, turning away from him is going to make things pretty ugly! That doesn't mean you won't necessarily be successful in the eyes of the world. You might be. But if you've made a regular habit of rebelling against God, you're going to be a mess on the *inside*. There's no way around it. I don't care how fabulous your life may seem to everyone else; if you knowingly and willfully and regularly indulge in behavior that goes contrary to the will of God and you're completely unrepentant, you're not going to be happy. It's impossible. Your inner life—and probably your family life as well—is going to suffer. It's an automatic consequence of turning away from the *source of all happiness*.

Now, if you've made a lifelong habit of rebelling against God and you're still not sorry—even at the point of death— there's going to be an automatic consequence. If you've rejected the grace God has freely given you; if you've refused to love him and your neighbors in the way that we're all called to do; if you've gotten to the end of the road and your attitude is still

"I don't care what God wants—it's what *I* want that matters";
then it's obvious what's going to happen when you die. You're
going to be standing there in front of God, all your sins exposed in the harsh light of truth, and by virtue of your own free
choice, you're going to immediately turn away from God—the
same way you did on earth.

That doesn't mean that God isn't going to issue some sort of
formal declaration of judgment. Scripture indicates that he
will. The point is that the soul being judged is going to be in *full
agreement* with God.

Here's a good way to understand how judgment works. Try
thinking about a time when you were indulging in a particular
sort of sin and you *knew* you were wrong, but you weren't ready
to stop. Maybe you intended to continue your behavior despite
any consequences and despite the fact that it was contrary to
your moral beliefs. Maybe you weren't sorry at all for your actions; or if you were, you weren't sorry enough to even *try* stop-
ping. When you were in that kind of state, how did you feel
spiritually? Did you feel very much like praying? Did you
feel like reading the Bible or going to church? What was your
general attitude toward things and activities that had to do with
God?

I bet you I know—I bet you wanted nothing to do with
them. I can tell you from my own experience that when I've
been in the grips of some particularly seductive sin and haven't
been very sorry, the *last* thing I wanted to do was think about
God. During those times I didn't want to see anything that remotely reminded me of God. If I was watching TV, for instance,
and I accidentally came across someone holding a Bible or

preaching, I couldn't switch channels fast enough. Thankfully, I don't experience that phenomenon quite as much as I used to, but I remember plenty of times in my life when I did. And by no means am I immune to it now.

Well, if you get to the end of your life and you're still stuck in that hardened, unrepentant, unfaithful state, the same kind of thing is going to happen again. You're going to see God and you're literally going to run in the opposite direction. The light of God isn't going to seem beautiful or warm or inviting to you. It's going to be painful. It's going to hurt. You're not even going to be able to look at it. You're going to want to get away from it as fast as you can. In fact, you're going to dive straight into hell! That's going to be your natural reaction. And God won't have to lift a finger.

The difference between turning away from God when you're alive on earth and doing it after your soul has separated from your body is that after death your action will be *irrevocable*. During your life, it's possible to fall and repent a billion times, and if you're truly sorry, God will forgive you. That's the essence of his mercy. But once you die, the time for repenting and "changing your mind" will be over. And the reason is, you'll no longer have a "mind" to change. Your soul, which previously had the power to choose between good and evil, will have made its *final* choice.

Remember what happened to the angels. They were created by God as pure spirits. Like human beings, they underwent a period of testing during which they had the opportunity to accept or reject God. But they didn't have to go back and forth a hundred times like we often do before choosing to do something.

They didn't experience their existence on a moment-to-moment basis as human beings do. Therefore, when they made their choice to go against God, it was instantaneous and permanent. They, too, couldn't "change their minds," because they had no minds to change. And there was nothing for them to "reconsider," because they never had to go through the process of "considering" in the first place. From the moment they were created, they had all the information they needed to make a decision about God. All they had to do was *choose*, once and for all.

Human beings find it extremely difficult to make irrevocable choices while on earth. We have the power to go back and forth constantly—and we use that power all the time. But eventually we're going to end up like the angels. At the moment of death, when our souls leave our bodies, all that will be left is the choice that we've made. And that choice will be either for God, or against him. And it will be fixed—forever.

God, of course, wants everyone to be with him in Heaven, and he's ready to forgive any sin, no matter how serious or how often it has been committed. I can't say it enough: one drop of Christ's blood is enough to wash away the sins of a *billion* universes. But if we've gotten to the end of our lives and we're still not sorry, there's really nothing God can do about it. He's not going to override our free will. He just doesn't do that. And this is really the meaning of the famous biblical passage about the "sin against the Holy Spirit"—which can't be forgiven. When a person rejects God's grace so completely that he can't bring himself to repent, even at the final hour, that person essentially condemns himself to hell. If at the point of death he insists on saying, "I will not believe. I will not love. I will not forgive. I

174 The Invisible World

will not be sorry," then what can God do? How can God forgive someone who doesn't want to be forgiven in the first place?

In addition to what happens to us at the moment of death, there's also something called the "Final Judgment," which is going to take place at the end of world. This is the scene Michelangelo painted so magnificently on the altar wall of the Sistine Chapel. It's also the frightening event that is often depicted in books and movies about the "Apocalypse." Sometimes it's called the "General Judgment." The Old Testament prophets referred to it on several occasions as the "Day of the Lord," and Christ himself foretold the event and graphically portrayed its circumstances in the Gospel of Matthew. The very last book of the Bible—the book of Revelation—is devoted to it.

We don't have the space here to adequately discuss this cataclysmic event. The Final Judgment really needs a separate chapter or a separate book all to itself. But because it's so important to the topic of invisible realities, let me sum up the basics.

Unlike the judgment that occurs immediately after we die—which is centered on the individual and is very much a private moment between us and God—the Final Judgment is going to be *public*. We all know that when Christ came to the earth the first time, two thousand years ago, he did it very quietly. The first Christmas took place in a shabby stable, with only the Virgin Mary, Saint Joseph, a few animals, and the silent stars as witnesses. That's not going to be the case the next time Christ comes. At the end of the world, Christ will be back in all his power and glory for everyone to see. And he's going to be here not as Redeemer, or teacher, or miracle worker—but as Judge.

The nature of the "judgment" he's going to make at that time will not be different from the one that's already been rendered at our death. Whether we go to Heaven or hell is determined the moment we die. And as we just said, it's basically a decision that we make ourselves—and one that isn't subject to change. At the Final Judgment all the questions we have about life are going to be answered. All the mysteries are at last going to be solved; all the "loose ends" will be tied up, all the blanks finally filled in. We're going to stand in front of God—all of us together, all the peoples of the earth from all times—and in a flash we're going to know the truth about ourselves, and the truth about one another. Every action of our lives is going to be "judged" for all to see—and we're going to be shown what all those actions led to. Whom did they help? Whom did they hurt? What good did we accomplish, and what evil? How much of our lives was substantive and worthwhile, and how much was vanity and fluff? Those are the kinds of things that are going to be evaluated and judged in the light of God's truth.

We're going to find out the answer to questions like Why did my mother die when I was so young? Why did my father get Alzheimer's disease? Why wasn't I able to have children? Why did my son get killed in a car accident? Why was I so lonely and depressed for so many years? What was the meaning of all my suffering? All of these questions and more are going to be answered. On that day, Saint John says, there will be no more questions to ask God.

And on the day of the Final Judgment we'll also experience the marvel of the Resurrection. This is one of those doctrines of the Christian faith that isn't emphasized as much as it should be. So many people have an overly spiritualized idea of the afterlife.

They think of Heaven and hell in terms that are much too vague and hazy. My first book, *A Travel Guide to Heaven*, was devoted to dispelling this myth, and it's worth taking a little time to focus on the ideas here. The most important thing to get clear is that human beings are meant to have bodies *and* souls—not just souls. We're not angels, and we're never going to be angels. When we go to Heaven, we don't turn into angels; and if we go to hell, we don't become demons. It's true that after we die our souls are going to be separated from our bodies, but that's only a temporary condition. On the day of the Final Judgment, our bodies and souls will once again be united—much in the same way that Christ's body and soul were reunited on the day of his Resurrection, the first Easter Sunday.

Recall that Christ died a brutal death on a cross. He underwent horrible suffering, and he experienced bodily death in the same exact way that you and I will. But when he rose from the dead, it wasn't just his spirit that came back to life. His body was brought back to life, too. It was his whole person. When he appeared to his apostles that first Easter morning, the same lungs that had been gasping for air on the cross were breathing again. The same muscles that had been wracked with pain were moving again. The same heart that had stopped on Good Friday was beating again.

And it's still beating today, in Heaven.

That's exactly what's going to happen to us. On the day of the Final Judgment we're going to be reunited with our bodies. They won't be completely the same, of course. They won't be old, for one—or infirm, or broken, or weak. They're going to be perfect. They're going to be what theologians call *glorified*. That means that our bodies are going to have certain kinds of amazing powers that even angels don't possess. No one knows for sure what those powers will be. But we have some idea. We know, for example, that the risen body will be so completely in synch with the soul that it will be possible for it to obey anything the soul commands. And that includes being able to travel anyplace, at any time, instantaneously—even across the length of the galaxy. It includes being able to live forever without getting old or weary or bored. It includes being able to experience joy and ecstasy with an intensity that would kill us if we experienced it today.

The Resurrection is one of the most comforting beliefs of Christianity. To know that you're eventually going to have a body in Heaven means that when you meet your departed friends and relatives there, you're going to be able to see them *in the flesh*. It means that if you're sad right now because your mother died, take heart! When you see her again in heaven, she won't be some kind of ghost. It will be *her*. You'll be able to run up to her and hug her and kiss her and feel the warmth of her skin and hear her voice again. That's what the Resurrection means. That's what awaits us in Heaven.

So many people think Heaven is going to be gray and white and cloudy. That couldn't be further from the truth. If we're destined to have physical bodies after the Resurrection, it means that Heaven itself is going to be physical—at least to some extent. After all, do you think our glorified bodies are going to spend eternity floating aimlessly through the air? Does that make any sense?

No, Heaven is going to be *real*. If you get anything out of this discussion, please let it be that. I don't know where you happen to be now as you're reading these words. Maybe you're in your bedroom, or sitting on a bus, or somewhere on vacation lounging on the beach. Wherever you are, take a quick look around you. Listen to the sounds. Breathe in the air. What you see and hear and smell is real. It's not a dream. What you absolutely must understand is that Heaven is going to be like that. It's not going to be less real than what you're experiencing now. If anything, it's going to be more real.

There's no reason to believe, for instance, that Heaven won't be bursting with color. There's no reason to think there won't be animals there—including every pet you ever owned. In fact, there's no reason to believe that Heaven isn't going to have all the natural beauties of our own world as well as many new kinds we haven't even dreamed of. And unlike the boring, static pictures that are often used to represent it, the real Heaven is going to be dynamic. It's going to be exciting, productive, fulfilling, and, yes, fun. And why shouldn't it be? If God is going to be in Heaven, and he's the source of all beauty, activity, life, and joy, then Heaven *must* be overflowing with all of those things. It's just common sense.

Does that mean our life in Heaven will be the same as our life on earth? Not at all. God never repeats himself in exactly the same way. He's much too original and creative an artist for that. And as Scripture clearly says, "No eye has seen, nor ear heard, nor the heart of man conceived, what God has prepared for those who love him." But no matter how different Heaven turns out to be, it's not going to be so radically different that we won't recognize it. When we get there, we're not going to feel as if we're in some kind of a strange, foreign land. On the contrary, we're going to feel as if we're home.

The same, unfortunately, can't be said about hell. It, too, is going to be every bit as real as the world we're living in now. But it won't feel like home at all.

A lot of people don't believe in hell. Not only is atheism on the rise today, but even Christians sometimes have their doubts about the existence of this infamous place where the damned go for all eternity. They just can't seem to bring themselves to believe that God would actually put anyone there—or that anyone would ever choose to go there himself.

Yet we've seen that it's very possible to rebel against God, and to do so obstinately. We know that Satan and many of the other angels chose to go to hell rather than serve God. And if they were able to make that kind of masochistic choice—and they're so much more brilliant and powerful than we are—why can't we? All you have to do is read a few history books or glance through the pages of the local newspaper, and you'll have all the evidence you'll ever need that people can choose evil over good. And you don't need to focus on Hitler and Stalin. Just look at the number of registered child molesters who are prowling every city of every country of the world.

The fact is, evil is all around us, evil so vile and shocking that it makes your skin crawl. I saw a story recently that almost made me physically ill. I hesitate to mention it, but I think it's important to acknowledge the presence of evil in our midst and not to sugarcoat it in any way or dismiss it all as psychological "sickness." The newspaper reported on a woman who lost patience with her little two-month-old baby because he was crying too much. In order to punish him, she didn't yell at him or spank him; she put him in a microwave oven—and turned it on.

Now, how in the world do you explain something so unbelievable? Of course the woman was mentally unbalanced. But there was more to it than that. There was something evil and sinister about her cruelty. Thank God someone was close by at the time and managed to save the child. But that doesn't make up for the monstrous thing she tried to do.

In the face of evil like this, it's hard to doubt the existence of hell. The Bible couldn't be more definitive on the matter. Both the Old and the New Testaments are full of references to it. Christ spoke about the horrors of hell on eleven separate occasions. Anyone who thinks hell doesn't really exist should go back and read those passages—they're among the most frightening in all Scripture. Christ didn't just mention hell. He used phrases like "everlasting fire," "outer darkness," "tormenting thirst," "a gnawing worm," and "weeping and gnashing of teeth." The fact that Our Lord devoted so much time to this subject—and in such a deadly serious way—shows that hell isn't just some kind of metaphor or literary device. No—hell is a real place, and people really go there.

What is hell like? We don't know very much, except that there's a great deal of suffering there. According to theologians, the greatest kind of pain in hell is simply being separated from God. Remember, God is Light and Joy and Peace. To turn away from him is to turn away from those things—permanently. It means plunging yourself into darkness, unhappiness, and chaos. And to have seen God—even just a glimpse of him at the moment of judgment—and then to withdraw from his presence, forever, knowing the kind of happiness you might have had, has got to be the most horrible kind of torment imaginable. After all, what is worse than the pain of loss?

You might ask: Is it possible to hate God and still feel intense suffering because of losing him and Heaven? Of course it is. It happens all the time in life. A person can have an enemy and still be jealous of his house and car and family and job and reputation. In fact, he might hate the other guy even more because of those things. He might get angrier and more depressed, knowing that he could never enjoy the kind of life his enemy has. His jealousy would literally eat away at him—even if he really, truly didn't want to spend any time in his enemy's company.

That's the way people in hell feel all the time. Only they're more belligerent about it. They know that their situation is never going to change, and they hate God all the more because of it. Remember, they blame him for everything—their suffering, their bitterness, their cruel destiny. And this sense of being cheated and abused only intensifies their misery.

I think one of the reasons that it's so hard to believe there are people in hell is because we have a tendency to view these poor folks as if they were just like us. As if they were a "mixture" of good and bad. And, yes, that may very well have been the case when they were on earth. It may have been what they were. But the truth is, people change when they go to hell. It's not so much that they become more evil; it's that they lose any of the good they once possessed. It's really the same thing that happens to people in Heaven, only in reverse. When you go to Heaven, you actually become *more* fully human; you become more of who you're *supposed* to be. Anytime you're in union with God, those natural virtues that God gave you are infused with his power. They're intensified, expanded. As a result, God's grace builds on your nature in such a way that you become a kind of "super version" of yourself. We talked about this earlier.

Well, when people go to hell, they become *less* themselves. In turning away from God, they essentially shut themselves off from his grace, and thus even the good they have shrivels up and disappears. C. S. Lewis had a great line about this. He said that what is cast into hell is not really a person but the "remains" of a person. It's what's left after the final, rebellious choice has been made and all the good has been drained out. Christ seemed to affirm this when he ominously said: "To him who has, more will be given . . . but from him who has not, even what he has will be taken away."

It's hard to imagine the kind of life these "human remains" will have in hell. If the "self" in Heaven is totally under the command of the will, it follows that in hell, the opposite must be true. Souls there must be self-centered in the extreme and completely dominated by their own antagonistic cravings and desires. It's hard enough keeping our appetites in check now. Just think how it would be if they were given free rein. That's what hell must be like—chaotic in the extreme—with all those frenzied, sinful desires warring with one another, and none of them under any control. Indeed, the only thing that unites the souls in hell is their shared hatred of God.

It's not a pleasant picture. And it becomes even more frightening when we consider the fact that after the Resurrection, the damned in hell are going to have *bodies*, too. The suffering they endure there won't just be spiritual in nature. It will be physical as well.

This is another thing people have trouble comprehending. They can't imagine what it would be like to be in pain *forever*. How can that be possible? But if you think about it, it really makes sense. If you spend your life abusing your body, it's going to eventually become wracked with pain. It's going to weaken and deteriorate to the point where even breathing hurts. What people don't realize is that when you rebel against God, your whole being suffers. And that includes your body. It doesn't matter what kind of exercise routine you may be on or how healthy you're eating. You may be going to the gym five times a week, lifting weights, running on the treadmill, taking your vitamins, and doing Yoga and Pilates. You may look great and feel great, and your doctor may even tell you that you're going to live to be a hundred. But that's only part of the story. There's something invisible going on, too. When you sin, you harm your body as well as your spirit. Sinning always results in disintegration and disorder. Always.

Why? Because the body is the temple of the Holy Spirit, and it's going to be affected physically if it rejects that Spirit. Consider what happens when a house is left vacant for a long period of time. Weeds grow, the paint peels, windows get broken, the wood rots away because of weather and termites, and everything starts falling apart. Well, that's the very same thing that happens to the human body when God stops living there. Only you don't see the physical deterioration in this life. You see it in the next.

There's a famous book called *The Picture of Dorian Gray*, by

Oscar Wilde, which captures some of what I'm trying to say here. The main character in the story is a corrupt young man named Dorian who sells his soul to the devil in order to keep his youthful beauty. The catch is that instead of Dorian growing old, his portrait must age. And that's exactly what happens. The young man begins living a life of selfish, hedonistic debauchery. He commits every sin imaginable. Sure enough, even though many years go by, his face and body remain unchanged. The portrait, however, begins to age terribly. And not only that, it begins to undergo disfigurement with every sin he commits. Before long, the painted face is hideous, with open sores and warts and pus-filled lesions and blotchy, scaly skin. It starts to actually resemble a monster—which is what Dorian has become.

The point of the story is that no matter how wonderful we may look on the outside, our evil actions do something to us. When we lead a life of sin, we suffer—both spiritually and physically—even though we may not realize it at the time. After the Resurrection, this will all be apparent. The souls in hell will rise to eternal life in the very same broken and decrepit bodies they created in life. And not only will those bodies be visible to everyone else, they'll feel pain. Not just because hell is a painful place, but because those bodies will be full of disease and wracked with pain.

I know, none of this is nice to think about. Believe me, it's not fun to write about either. But if we're going to talk about the invisible things that happen to us when we die, we have to include both the good and the bad. We can't afford to go through life with spiritual blinders on. We're all headed in the same direction—toward death—and the likelihood is that we're going to get there sooner than we think.

When that finally happens—when it's time for us to depart this world of ours and meet our maker—isn't it better that we have some idea of what to expect? When that moment of moments finally arrives, and all the hidden spiritual realities that we've been speaking about—angels, demons, the devil, even God himself—become visible to us for the first time, wouldn't it be better to be prepared? I think so.

The question is, do we really have to wait till that day to see all these spiritual realities? Is there a way, perhaps, for us to make the spiritual world visible while we're on this side of the grave? A way that bypasses the physical limitations of our eyes? A way that doesn't involve the occult or nonsense such as séances and tarot cards?

What if I told you there were special kinds of "eyeglasses" you could wear that would give you this power? Eyeglasses that have "divine" lenses. What if when you put these glasses on, the whole invisible world suddenly came to life before your eyes? Not only would that give you an incredible foretaste of what awaits you in the next life, but it would also assist you to know exactly what to do and how to act in this life.

Well, I've got news for you. It *is* possible. No, I don't have a set of magic eyeglasses to give you. But I can tell you about the spiritual equivalent. There is a way to "see" the invisible without using your eyes, and it's not as complicated as you might imagine.

And that's the subject of our next and last chapter.

CHAPTER 10

SEEING THE INVISIBLE

Every year at Christmastime, newspapers across America reprint an editorial that was written back in 1897 called "Yes Virginia, There Is a Santa Claus" Most people are familiar with the story behind the article. A little girl had sent a letter to the New York *Sun* saying that her friends didn't believe in Santa anymore, and she wanted the newspaper to tell her the truth: Was he real or just imaginary? The editor, Francis Church, took the opportunity to answer a much bigger question, about the existence of invisible realities. In a very a simple but profound way, he said to her:

> *Virginia, your little friends are wrong. They have been affected*
> *by the skepticism of a skeptical age. They do not believe except*
> *[what] they see. They think that nothing can be which is not*
> *comprehensible by their little minds. All minds, Virginia,*
> *whether they be men's or children's, are little. . . . You may tear*
> *apart the baby's rattle and see what makes the noise inside, but*
> *there is a veil covering the unseen world which not the strongest*
> *man . . . could tear apart. Only faith, fancy, poetry, love,*
> *romance, can push aside that curtain and view and picture the*
> *supernal beauty and glory beyond. Is it all real? Ah, Virginia,*
> *in all this world there is nothing else real and abiding. . . .*

In this book, we've tried to pull back the "veil covering the unseen world" just a little, so we could glimpse some of life's invisible realities. We haven't covered all of them—it would take many books to do that. But we have talked about the essential ones, the ones that have the most bearing on our day-to-day lives. The only question that remains for us now is how can we see those realities more clearly? Is there a way for us to visualize them in a more concrete manner?

And the answer is yes, there most certainly is. In the last chapter I brought up the possibility of wearing special spiritual eyeglasses. Eyeglasses with "divine lenses." In this chapter I want to explore that metaphor more fully. I'd like to actually show you how to make a pair of these glasses. Believe it or not, it's not very hard to do. It doesn't require any miraculous powers. It isn't expensive. It doesn't matter how knowledgeable or ignorant you happen to be of spiritual matters. If you're a human being, and you're open to doing God's will, you can put these glasses together. And if you "wear" them on a regular basis, I guarantee that the invisible world we've been discussing will come into focus in a way you never before imagined.

Regular eyeglasses have four basic parts: the frame, the lenses, the bridge over the nose, and the sidepieces that extend to behind the ears. The special glasses we're going to talk about have four basic parts, too. And these parts correspond to four practical things anyone can do. The first three are very basic, and I'll sum them up quickly. The fourth is a bit more complex. But all are extremely effective in helping you see the spiritual realities around you.

And by seeing, of course, I don't mean seeing with your

eyes. Invisible realities are invisible for a reason. It's their nature to be unseen, and that's the way God wants it. What I mean is seeing with *God's eyes*; viewing the world the way he views it; believing that worldview with every fiber of your being, and then acting on it. That's authentic spiritual vision.

How can you do that? Well, the first way is very simple. So simple, in fact, that it's often overlooked. If you want to see the invisible world that God has created, the most fundamental thing to do is ask God to help you to see it. In other words, you can pray. You can say, "Lord, please make me more aware of what you're doing in my life. Help me to know when your angels are assisting me, when demons are trying to tempt me, when you're sending me your graces, when you're leading me in a certain direction, when my suffering has meaning."

Why is it so necessary to pray in this way? Because God is Light—and you need light in order to see. And God is Wisdom—and you need wisdom in order to understand what you're seeing. Without light and understanding, it's impossible to see anything in this world. You'd basically be blind. And that's the way so many people go through life—blind.

Luckily, this condition doesn't have to be permanent. Some of the most wonderful miracles in the Bible have to do with God giving sight to the blind. That's really what we're asking him to do here. When you pray to God to help you see the invisible, you're essentially asking him to cure you of your "spiritual blindness." And if you do that every day, God is going to answer you. That doesn't mean that angels are going to start magically appearing on your doorstep, but you can be sure that the whole spiritual realm is going to become much more real to you in a very short time. Just try it and see if it doesn't work.

Another basic thing you can do to see the invisible is to read about it. There happens to be a very famous book that God wrote called the Bible! In this book you can find out all about God's invisible activities over the course of thousands of years. You can see and hear God speaking—not just to prophets and kings and saints but to you, personally. If the spiritual world has never been very real to you, or if for some reason it has grown stale, the best thing to do is to open up the Bible and dive right in. Any section will do, but the last part—the New Testament—is especially valuable because it's the place where God is most clearly visible, the place where you can see God walking, talking, living, and breathing, in the person of Jesus Christ. For me, personally, the Gospel of Luke has always been a fine place to start. It's not as short or direct as the Gospel of Mark, its theology isn't as sublime or profound as the Gospel of John, and it doesn't have as many of Jesus's sayings as the Gospel of Matthew. But for sheer beauty and simplicity of writing, nothing beats it.

A third simple way you can see the invisible—and a very powerful way at that—is by helping the poor. We can't ever forget that God didn't just lounge around Heaven after he created us, twiddling his divine thumbs. He got *busy*. He jumped right into human history and started mixing it up with us. He became a man in order to help us. He wasn't afraid to get his hands dirty, so to speak, and neither should we be. There are lots of people out there who need our help. Lots of people who are

suffering badly. And it's our job to assist them. Every single
one of us is called to give and give until it hurts. When Christ
said, "Blessed are the pure in heart—*for they shall see God*," he was
mainly talking about being selfless. He was talking about the
need to give of ourselves without being concerned about the cost
or about what we might get in return. A pure heart is one that
isn't overly contaminated with self-interest. It's one that has a
single-minded focus on doing God's will. Thus, if you really
want to see God, one of the surest ways is to begin carrying out
some of the so-called "corporal works of mercy"—feeding the
hungry, giving drink to the thirsty, clothing the naked, shelter-
ing the homeless, comforting the imprisoned, and visiting the
sick. If you do these things, I guarantee that your heart will
become more pure. It has to. There's just no way that vanity
and selfishness can grow in an environment of such terrible
suffering. And with your new, purified heart you'll begin to see
all kinds of marvelous and mysterious things you never noticed
before.

So much for the basics. So much for the bridge, frame, and
sidepieces of this special pair of eyeglasses. The fourth "part"—
the divine lenses themselves—requires a more lengthy explanation. But it's worth it, because it's one of the cornerstones of
Christian spirituality. In fact, if you do nothing else but try to
put into practice the ideas we're going to discuss in the next few
pages, I promise that your life will undergo a radical transformation. Because what I'm about to tell you is really the secret
to unlocking the whole hidden universe of the spirit.

If you want to see the invisible, then you have to *be* invisible.
Let me explain.

There was an old black-and-white movie that used to scare me when I was a kid called *The Incredible Shrinking Man*. It was about a man who is accidentally exposed to some kind of strange radioactive cloud, and as a result starts to get smaller. First he hardly notices the change, except for the fact that his clothes are too large for him. But by the end of the movie, he's no bigger than an ant. Despite its campiness (there are battle scenes between him and a cat, a spider, and so on), the film really isn't too bad. In fact, the concept is kind of interesting. As the man shrinks and becomes "invisible" to those around him, he begins to notice all kinds of incredible things that are "invisible" to everyone else.

And that's the point. When you're little, you see a lot that's hidden from the rest of the world. Christ said, "Unless you change and become like little children, you will never enter the Kingdom of Heaven." What did he mean by that? He certainly wasn't saying that we should become children again, in the literal sense. No, he was talking about *spiritual childhood*. He was talking about humility. When you make yourself small and humble to the point of being self-forgetful, a whole new world opens up to you—God's world.

Being a child spiritually means many things. It means that you completely understand your "littleness" before God. It means that no matter how intelligent you are, no matter how good-looking you are, no matter how talented you are, you understand that you're nothing compared to God—and you're nothing without God. It means that when you approach God or anything connected to him, you don't do it with an arrogant spirit. Sometimes even Scripture scholars and theologians forget this.

They forget that when you study the subject of theology, you must do so *on your knees*. And so their pride sometimes causes them to fall into terrible errors—errors so basic that even the most uneducated believers dismiss them out of hand.

Being a child spiritually also means that you don't have to do anything "great" in order to become a great saint. You don't have to be a martyr. You don't have to experience ecstasies. You don't need to receive any special revelations. You don't have to perform any heroic deeds. If God gives you the opportunity to accomplish great things for the faith, fine. But if he doesn't, that's just as well. The point is that every action you take, no matter how small and ordinary, should be done for the love of God. If you start each morning by saying, "God, I'm just a poor sinner, but all that I do today I do for you," then the entire day will be sanctified. Washing dishes, brushing your teeth, reading a book, walking the dog, putting up with an obnoxious coworker—everything will have meaning. Even the most menial task, if done for the love of God, will have immense, supernatural value in God's eyes.

Being a child spiritually means that you *expect* to make mistakes and fall into sin. After all, you're a weak, sinful human being. You're not perfect, and you're never going to be perfect. When you're truly humble, you're never surprised or shocked when you commit a sin—even if it's an extremely serious sin, and even if you commit the same sin a thousand times. That doesn't mean you're not sorry, or that you're not committed to changing. It just means that you fully recognize the truth that you don't have any real power or strength apart from what God gives you.

Believe me, if you fall into despair over some offense that you've committed, it's a sure sign of pride. It's a sign that you think you're stronger than you actually are. If you were truly humble, you would never beat yourself up. You would *pick yourself up*, say you're sorry, and try not to do it again. Period. You would never get too upset, and you would never, ever lose hope, because you would understand how weak and little you really are.

Being a child spiritually means that as long as you're legitimately trying to do God's will, you'll never be afraid of him. People are sometimes scared that God isn't going to love them anymore because of all the sins they've committed. Or they're petrified that he's going to hurl some sort of lightning bolt at them. How silly! A wise person once asked, How could anyone be afraid of a God who became a little baby?

Exactly! You have to have absolute, supreme, and unconditional confidence in God's mercy. And you have to *act* like you do, too. Let's say you have a child who did something very naughty. What if you came home from work and this child immediately went off into the corner and started to sulk? What if, instead of apologizing, he tried to stay as far away from you as he could? What if he just avoided you out of fear or out of an unwillingness to face the consequences of his actions? Behavior like that wouldn't make you any less upset with him, would it? You'd probably still go through the whole routine of calling him over, asking him if he understood what he did wrong, and possibly even punishing him. After all that's what parents normally do.

Now what if this child had done something completely dif-

ferent? What if the moment you walked through the door he
ran up to you and jumped into your arms and hugged you as
tightly as he could, and said, "Mommy [or Daddy], I did something wrong, but I love you and I'm very sorry." And what if,
after apologizing, he kept giving you kisses and hugs? And
what if he was really sincere, and not just trying to manipulate
you? How would you feel? Wouldn't it be hard to be angry at a
child like that? Wouldn't it be next to impossible to stay mad at
anyone who showed so much sincere contrition and trust and
love and abandonment?

Well, that's the way you should *always* act when you offend
God.

You see, being a child spiritually is all about how you approach God. It's all about recognizing your shortcomings, accepting them, and humbly asking for God's forgiveness and
help. It's about accepting the fact that you're not a free agent,
that you're truly dependent upon God every moment of every
day for everything. Just as a child is dependent on his parents.

And this dependence extends even beyond God—to the
whole community of believers. Being a child spiritually means
you're not so arrogant that you think that you can "do it all
alone." Because you can't! To be a Christian means that you're
part of a family. How so?

Remember the story of "Doubting Thomas"? When Jesus
appeared to his disciples in the "upper room" after he had risen
from the dead, the apostle Thomas wasn't with them. He was
out somewhere. When he returned and was told about the Lord's
mysterious visit, he didn't believe them. He said, famously, "Unless I see in his hands the print of the nails, and place my finger

in the mark of the nails, and place my hand in his side, I will not believe." A week later the disciples were gathered together again, and this time Thomas was with them. The doors were shut, and Jesus suddenly appeared in their midst and went straight up to Thomas and said, "Put your finger here, and see my hands; and put out your hand, and place it in my side." It was only then that Thomas got down on his knees and said, "My Lord and my God!"

Now, the first question that always comes to my mind when I read this Gospel passage is, Where was Thomas when Christ made his first appearance? Remember, the apostles were a very tight-knit group of men, hardly ever out of one another's company. Why was he missing? Some scholars have speculated that because Thomas had an inquisitive, almost cynical nature, he may have been out looking for Jesus. Knowing that the Lord's body was missing from the tomb, and also that Jesus had supposedly appeared to Mary Magdalene and others, he may very well have gone out looking for Christ himself, making inquiries, checking facts, searching to find the answer to the mystery. Of course, he found nothing.

To me that's the key point. When did Thomas actually see the Lord? Only when he was with the community of believers. When he was out by himself, he came up empty-handed. But when he was together with his fellow apostles—with those who made up the early Church—Jesus appeared to him, visibly. That's when Thomas not only saw Jesus with his eyes, but saw clearly with his mind and soul the truth about the Lord. For Thomas was the very first person to state explicitly that Jesus *was* God.

Something similar happened to the Holy Family twenty years earlier. Recall that when Jesus was a little boy there was a three-day period when he went missing. Mary and Joseph had taken him on their annual trip to Jerusalem for the Passover feast, and suddenly they couldn't find him. He had disappeared. Naturally they were frantic. They searched high and low but no one knew where he was. Finally, they went back to the Temple and to their great relief, they saw him—right in the middle of a group of rabbis. That's where he had been all along, with those who were teaching and learning and praying and reading Scripture. When they told Jesus they had been looking for him, he merely responded, "Did not you know that I had to be in my Father's house?"

Both these passages have to do with God's being "invisible." And both show that the way to "see" him is to spend time among the community of believers. There's a definite communal component to Christianity, and it can't be ignored. When Jesus taught people to pray, he didn't tell them to say "My Father, who art in heaven," he told them to say *"Our* Father." Likewise, he said to his disciples, "Where *two or three* are gathered in my name—there am I in the midst of them." Believing in God, despite what it may seem, is not strictly a one-on-one affair. It involves everyone. Having a personal relationship with the Lord—which is something everyone needs—is never an excuse for self-absorption and self-centeredness. It's not an accident that the symbol of our faith is not a circle or some other closed figure but a cross, with its beams extending outward in all directions—North, South, East, and West. To be a Christian, by definition, means to go *out* of yourself, rather than to retreat inward.

The last and most important quality of spiritual childhood is also the most important thing in life: the necessity of having childlike faith.

Faith is the key to seeing the invisible. In fact, it's the key to everything. You can pray, read the Bible, help the poor, try to be humble, and worship with the community of believers all you want, but if you don't have a childlike faith, the invisible world is going to remain very obscure to you. Some people, of course, claim that they can't bring themselves to have faith, no matter how hard they try. I've never understood this. Everybody has faith. They have to. It's impossible to live without it.

For example, I get up every day at five a.m. and drive to work. During my commute, nothing separates me from oncoming traffic except a thin white line. Each morning I pass hundreds of cars and trucks—all of them coming right at me and going over sixty miles and hour. If just one of those vehicles swerved a few feet to my right, I would be dead. Yet I don't even blink when they whizz past me on the highway. Why? Do I know those drivers? Do I know their driving records? Do I know whether they're watching the road or whether they're so preoccupied with their own problems that they don't even see me? Do I know if any of them has a drinking problem? No, I don't know anything. And yet I drive merrily along. Why? Because I have *faith* that those other drivers are going to stick to their side of the road.

When I get to work it's the same thing. I sit down at my

desk and right over my head is a ceiling. In all the years I've been working in my office I've never once gotten up on a ladder and inspected it. I haven't checked to see if the support beams are nailed in properly or if the wood has been eaten away by termites. For all I know, the whole roof might suddenly collapse and crush me. And yet day after day I sit there in front of my computer screen without a care in the world. Why? Do I know any of the carpenters or workers who originally constructed the building? Do I know if all the building permits are in order? No, I don't know anything! The only reason I can do my work in peace is because I have faith that the people who built my office were professionals and did everything they were supposed to do.

Everything in life comes down to faith. Our whole knowledge of human history is based on it. Think about it. Were you around when the Romans conquered Carthage in 146 BC? How about when Columbus discovered America in 1492? Do you know for sure that George Washington crossed the Delaware River in 1776? No? Well, how do you know those events took place?

Oh, but there's "evidence," you say. There are documents and books and testimonies and paintings. That's right, there are. And that's the very same "evidence" we have that Jesus Christ performed miracles and rose from the dead. There's really no difference. Yes, it's true that some pieces of evidence may be more "convincing" than others, but the bottom line is that it's all based on information that has been passed down to us from generation to generation. None of it is firsthand. None of it is scientifically provable. All of it, really, must be accepted on faith—faith in the authors of the documents, and faith in the reliability of the testimonies.

If anything, the Christian position has more compelling evidence to back it up. There's the witness of the early martyrs—thousands of men, women, and children who went to their deaths refusing to recant their testimony about the Resurrection; there's the evidence of supernatural revelation—all the millions upon millions of miracles that have taken place over the centuries as a result of faith in Christ; there are all the philosophical, moral, and logical arguments that have been put forward by the most brilliant thinkers who ever lived. In other words, there's more than enough "evidence" to justify having faith in God and his Son.

Believe it or not, even atheists have faith. They may not admit it, but they do. After all, they believe that this universe of ours—a universe of unparalleled beauty, harmony, and order—came about all by itself. They believe that life came about all by itself. Bear in mind, the statistical odds that even the most elemental kind of life could arise as the result of the random mixing of molecules in some sort of primordial "soup" are so astronomical that even scientists can't figure them out. They can't say, for instance, that the odds are "trillions to one," because that figure is too small! Yet atheists obstinately refuse to accept even the possibility of a "Creator." Their position contradicts logic, contradicts experience, it even contradicts science, yet they still believe it. That takes faith!

Christians don't have that problem. Our position is flawlessly logical. If there's a watch, there must be a watchmaker. And if the universe and the human body are infinitely more complicated than a watch, then they, too, must have a "maker" of some kind.

The agnostic position attempts to get around all this and avoid the responsibility (and obligation) of making a choice. The agnostic says: "I'm not against believing in God. But I'm not sure. You'll have to *show* me first. If you show me, then I'll believe."

Well, I'm afraid that's not the way God operates. God is all about freedom. He's all about empowerment. Of course, he could make a huge, blazing cross appear in the sky. And then everyone would have no choice but to believe in his existence. But he doesn't want to force us to do anything. He doesn't want us to act the morally correct way because we "have to." If God were to appear magically in the clouds, we would probably do whatever he told us to do—but only because we were afraid that if we didn't, he would "get us." That's not what God had in mind.

No, God gives us all the evidence we need to make a free choice—all the evidence of nature and logic and common sense and reliable testimonies and revelation. Then he leaves it up to us to decide. That's why faith is not, ultimately, a feeling but rather a decision. An informed, intelligent decision. But a decision nonetheless.

And it's a decision that should be made earlier rather than later. In this crazy, unpredictable world of ours, you never know when "later" is going to come. I used to have an uncle I was very fond of. He was a real character. A gruff, tough-talking Italian, impatient, opinionated, with absolutely no tolerance for anyone who was incompetent or wasted time—especially *his* time. On the local level, he wielded a good deal of political influence and controlled many jobs, so he was considered a powerful man. And he knew it. Yet underneath the harsh, cursing exterior he could be very kindhearted, and over the years he helped an awful lot of people—many times quietly.

Well, one day this uncle of mine got cancer, and it was the very worst kind. The doctors gave him no more than a year to live. There was absolutely no chance of survival, they said. It was a death sentence, plain and simple. Being an extremely worldly individual—his whole life devoted to his job and politics—the news of the cancer, coming so suddenly and unexpectedly, dealt him a blow he couldn't withstand. He literally crumbled under the weight of it. To say he was terrified would be an understatement. He was absolutely panic-stricken for months. During that time my father, who was his older brother, visited him every day at his house, and they had many conversations. At first my uncle was too scared to even mention the subject of death. All his thoughts, emotions, and efforts were focused on trying to figure out a way to beat the cancer. Eventually, though, when it became apparent that this was one opponent he wasn't going to politically outmaneuver, he settled into a sustained period of agony and fear. Many things frightened him. The nighttime, the darkness, being alone, the intense suffering he knew was coming, death itself, the prospect of nothingness—the possibility of judgment.

The greatest source of anxiety for him, however, was his lack of certainty regarding spiritual matters. Early in his life he had been a believer, but after the death of his mother and a few other tragedies he had fallen away from the faith. Then, like the seeds in the Gospel story that fell among thorny bushes, he became entangled in worldly affairs and ambitions, and whatever faith he had left was choked out. Now, in the final hour of his life, he was forced to go back and rethink everything. It was very difficult for him to do. He was a brilliant man, extremely analytical and logical. His common sense told him there had to be a God, but his need to dissect and understand everything held him back from embracing the faith. So his mind circled round and round the idea of God and Heaven and eternal life, but he couldn't bring himself to accept these things wholeheartedly. He just didn't know if they were true or not, and his inability to come to a definite conclusion tortured him.

Finally, after one of their long conversations in which my uncle kept saying, "I don't know, I don't know, I don't know," my father stopped him and said forcefully: "Enough thinking and analyzing. Just believe! *Just believe!*"

And you know what? That worked. After that conversation, my uncle finally started to experience some peace. He told my father a week or so later that he was actually able to sleep at night; that he had made up his mind to have faith, and he felt much better. He knew it wasn't a blind faith. He knew it was based on reason and common sense. But he also understood that it was time to stop circling. It was time to make a choice. And he did. He ended up facing death with great courage, great peace, and great manly fortitude—the same kind he had displayed so often in life.

What my father said to my uncle helped him to stop making an endless loop and finally make a decision. And once again, that's what faith is—a decision. Everyone is given the gift *to be able to believe*. But we still have to make the choice ourselves.

And the choice is to accept or reject God. In the end, that's what life comes down to. All the facts we need to make our choice are readily at hand. All the testimonies are in. All the arguments, pro and con, have been made—a million times over. Now it's up to us to decide.

My hope for you as we come to the end of this book is that you make that decision—once and for all, and in the affirmative. Not only that God exists, but that the invisible world exists, too. A vibrant, living, dynamic world—a world of mystery, but a world every bit as real as the one we're familiar with.

What is this strange world like? Imagine for a moment that you really had a pair of these eyeglasses we've been talking about. Eyeglasses with divine lenses, specially crafted by God, which would bring into focus all of life's spiritual realities. If you were to put these glasses on right now and walk out of your house, what would you see?

I'll tell you. You'd see millions and millions of angels. Angels all around you. On busses, in cars, on the street, in the office, everywhere there are human beings. Not the cute, cartoonish figures with halos and wings that appear on television shows or in department store windows, but real, live, spiritual beings with immense power—beings whose main objective is to help us get to Heaven. You'd see them assisting people in their daily lives, talking softly in their ears, encouraging them, warning them, helping them to avoid sins.

You'd see the fallen angels as well. The demons of hell. Frightening, hellish creatures. Angry, prideful, resentful of God, hateful toward human beings. You'd see them doing Satan's bidding, trying just as hard as the angels to influence people's decisions, tempting them, enticing them, seducing them, lying to them, doing everything they can to turn people away from God.

You'd see for the first time that the people you meet on the street every day aren't just people—but immortal beings. Beneath their suits and ties and dresses and jeans and makeup and lipstick and shoes, you'd see that they have invisible souls, meant to live for all eternity, and that they have a value and a dignity far greater than all the stars and planets in the universe put together.

When these people prayed, you would see how their requests immediately went up to Heaven, like beams of white light. And you'd see God's graces flooding back down to earth upon their heads, giving them the help they need to follow his will. You'd see the spiritual trajectory of human words and actions—how each has consequences that extend far into the future and eternity. You'd also see the real effect of lies and sins, and how they cause disorder in the universe and disintegration in the whole fabric of existence.

You'd see the power of Christ-like suffering—all the millions of graces that are released into the world every time a person endures even the smallest amount of pain for God's sake. You'd see the truth about what happens at the moment of death—how guardian angels escort the souls of the blessed to Paradise and how demons taunt and torture the souls of the damned as they flee from God's presence into the black, oppressive darkness of hell.

You'd look toward Heaven, and you'd see the faces of all

your loved ones who have died. All the people who left you over the years, one by one, and who you thought were gone forever. You'd see them, standing there, smiling, happy beyond words, and waiting for the day when they'll be able to embrace you and kiss you and speak to you again, in the same way they did on earth.

You'd see *him*, too. The one who created you and created the whole world. The source of all life and joy and truth. You'd see him face-to-face. Not just the bright "light" you hear about in movies and television shows and books, but the actual God of Power and Might. The First Uncaused Cause. The Beatific Vision. The Blessed Trinity.

At the mere sight of him your soul would be infused with an ecstasy so great and overwhelming that you wouldn't be able to survive, if he himself didn't use his powers to keep you alive. And the amazing thing is that when you looked at this Being, you wouldn't just be seeing a spirit—you'd be seeing *a man*. The same man who was born in a stable in Bethlehem that first Christmas morning two thousand years ago. The same man who lived and walked and taught among us. And if you looked at this man closely enough, you would see the very same nail marks in his hands and feet that he received the day of his crucifixion.

We talked a little before about "Doubting Thomas," the apostle who refused to believe in the risen Christ until he had seen those nail marks with his own eyes and touched them with his own fingers. But we didn't finish the story. When Christ appeared in the upper room and showed Thomas the holes in his hands and feet, and the apostle got on his knees and exclaimed,

"My Lord and my God!" Christ said something to him that has rung down through the ages and speaks to all of us today who live in this cynical, skeptical age. He said:

*"Thomas, because thou hast seen me, thou hast believed.
Blessed are they that have not seen, and yet have believed."*

One of the greatest tragedies in life is to disbelieve in the existence of the invisible world or to ignore it altogether. If you do that—if you insist on seeing only with your physical eyes, if you make your five senses into five tyrannical little dictators, if you worship science as the be-all and end-all of everything— then you're doomed to live only half a life. And the half you do live is sure to be devoid of any real, lasting meaning.

Don't make that mistake. By all means question and learn and study and analyze. But do it with a humble spirit. If you have doubts, don't be arrogant about them. Don't be a scoffer. Try as hard as you can to become a child spiritually. Forget about yourself and your problems—even if just for a little while. Go to where the poor are and help them. Give of yourself completely. Then go where other believers are and pray with them. Worship with them. Receive the sacraments with them. And then close your eyes and say to God, "Lord, I still don't understand life. I don't understand you. But help me. If you're there, I want to know you. I want to see you. I want to see what's hidden behind the veil that covers the unseen world."

Then when you've done all that, open your eyes. Not the ones in your head—but the ones in your soul.

And just believe.

About the Author

Anthony DeStefano is the bestselling author of *A Travel Guide to Heaven, Ten Prayers God Always Says Yes To,* and the children's books *This Little Prayer of Mine* and *Little Star.* He lives in New York.